MAKING ASSESSMENT MATTER

Making
Assessment
Matter

**Using Test Results
to Differentiate Reading
Instruction**

Nonie K. Lesaux
Sky H. Marietta

THE GUILFORD PRESS
New York   London

© 2012 The Guilford Press
A Division of Guilford Publications, Inc.
72 Spring Street, New York, NY 10012
www.guilford.com

Printed in the United States of America

This book is printed on acid-free paper.

Last digit is print number: 9 8 7 6 5 4 3 2 1

Library of Congress Cataloging-in-Publication Data

Lesaux, Nonie K.
   Making assessment matter: using test results to differentiate reading
instruction / Nonie K. Lesaux, Sky H. Marietta.
      p. cm.
   Includes bibliographical references and index.
   ISBN 978-1-4625-0246-2 (pbk.) — ISBN 978-1-4625-0248-6 (hardcover)
   1. Reading—Remedial teaching. 2. Reading (Elementary) 3. Reading—
Ability testing. 4. Educational tests and measurements. 5. Individualized
instruction. 6. Learning disabled children. 7. Response to intervention
(Learning disabled children) I. Marietta, Sky H. II. Title.
   LB1050.5.L3878 2012
   372.43—dc23
                                                        2011035023

To the students, educators, and instructional leaders
with whom we have been fortunate to work over the years

Their hard work as learners, teachers, and leaders
is reflected in the stories we share in these pages.

About the Authors

Nonie K. Lesaux, PhD, is Marie and Max Kargman Associate Professor in Human Development and Urban Education Advancement at the Harvard Graduate School of Education, where she teaches graduate courses in reading development and difficulties, and leads a research program that focuses on increasing opportunities to learn for students from diverse linguistic, cultural, and economic backgrounds. Dr. Lesaux's research is conducted in partnership with large school districts and Head Start programs, and supported by grants from several organizations, including the Institute of Education Sciences, the Eunice Kennedy Shriver National Institute of Child Health and Human Development, the Administration for Children and Families, the Council of the Great City Schools, and the William and Flora Hewlett Foundation. She was Senior Research Associate of the National Literacy Panel on Language Minority Youth. In 2007, Dr. Lesaux received a William T. Grant Scholars Award in support of her research on English language learners in urban public schools. She is also a recipient of a Presidential Early Career Award for Scientists and Engineers, the highest honor given by the U.S. government to young professionals beginning their independent research careers.

Sky H. Marietta, EdM, MAT, is a doctoral candidate at the Harvard Graduate School of Education and a former elementary school teacher. As an educator, Ms. Marietta taught in public schools on the Navajo Nation in New Mexico, where she received her master's degree in teaching. Her program of research aims to improve student achievement by exploring the diversity in the language and literacy experiences of children living in poverty. She has been involved in administering assessments and analyzing child outcomes in oral language and literacy skills in varied contexts, including Early Head Start centers and public schools in rural and urban settings. She has applied her understanding of child assessment and instruction to developing and presenting professional development materials on data-driven literacy instruction. As a teacher educator, Ms. Marietta has taught classes on language and culture. She has also supervised master's students in Reading Specialist and Elementary Counseling licensure programs.

Acknowledgments

We have many people and organizations to thank, for their professional partnerships and collaborations and for their intellectual investment and support in seeing this information and our ideas disseminated. There are a number of school sites we've worked with, independently and together, whose partnerships are reflected here. Primarily, these are district leaders, principals, and teachers in the Boston Public Schools and in the San Diego Unified School District. Special thanks go to Jason Sachs and Ben Russell of the Boston Public Schools for their involvement and support of this work, and for the link to Valora Washington and the CAYL Principal Fellowship. In the San Diego Unified School District, we thank Carol Barry and Teresa Walters for their support of research that garnered insights important to this work, especially as it relates to students from linguistically diverse backgrounds. We also thank Hiro Yoshikawa, Rick Weissbourd, and other members of the Harvard-based PreK–3rd program. Chris Jennison, former Publisher of Education at The Guilford Press, gave Nonie impetus to take on this writing project, and his enthusiasm and support for the work propelled the effort forward. A Scholars Award from the William T. Grant Foundation provided time for Nonie to devote to this writing project; for that support, and the Foundation's ongoing training and commitment in the area of brokering knowledge for policymakers and practitioners, she is especially grateful. Rose K. Vukovic, Nonie's friend and colleague at the NYU Steinhardt School of Culture, Education, and Human Development, provided important clarity on some of the issues presented here. At Harvard, we thank all members of the Language Diversity and Literacy Development Research Group: Julie Russ, Joan Kelley, Armida Lizarraga, Rebecca Givens Rolland, Jennifer Jacoby, Beth Faller, Christina Dobbs, Rachel Slama, Emma Billard, Perla Gamez, and Michelle Hastings. Special thanks to Julie Russ, Joan Kelley, and Armida Lizarraga for their especially close reading of the manuscript. Finally, we acknowledge the support of our respective partners, Scott Furlong and Geoff Marietta, and acknowledge the role that Harlan Marietta played in anchoring this work in real life; he was taking his very first assessment (the APGAR) on the day the proposal for this book was accepted for publication.

Contents

MAKING ASSESSMENT MATTER

PART I

Foundational Issues
for Data-Driven Instruction

CHAPTER 1

A New Relationship with Student Data

Introduction to Our Case Site: Rosa Parks Elementary

Outside it was a lovely evening, but the warmth of autumn twilight went unnoticed inside the aging brick building that housed Rosa Parks Elementary. Principal Mary Lansdowne and her dedicated staff, already fatigued from a long day of teaching, were poring over the state test results and shaking their heads. News had already spread that the school had not fared well. The data were particularly disappointing because this year they had pushed—really pushed—to avoid the scores they were now facing. Overall, Principal Lansdowne had a dedicated, caring, and knowledgeable team. Yet despite what they considered their best effort, the reading scores of their third, fourth, and fifth graders had stayed low. Their English language learners' (ELLs) scores were actually lower than the previous year's scores. "I don't understand," said a third-grade teacher, her frustration visible. "I know my kids. They know how to read and they're good learners. What is happening here?"

Principal Lansdowne understood why her teachers were frustrated. The staff at Rosa Parks Elementary had become skilled at evaluating student data and had implemented initiatives to promote data-driven instruction. They gathered for data meetings to carefully analyze annual state test results. Three times a year, substitute teachers were brought into the building so that teachers could individually assess each child's reading skills. To the teachers and to Principal Lansdowne, too, the assessment process felt comprehensive. It followed a procedure that made sense to them: Each student read passages while the teacher marked errors; at the end of passages students were asked comprehension questions. If a student did well, he or she would move to a harder text; if a student really struggled, he or she moved to an easier passage. This would continue until the reading level of the student was identified. The reading levels were used to group the students and help them choose their "just right" books in classroom libraries for independent reading. On top of that, there were regular grade-level meetings where teachers discussed the students whose performances were most worrisome. Apart from all this careful work done during the school year, this past summer they spent hours juggling schedules to ensure that the lowest-performing students received additional support, including an intricately crafted tutoring schedule.

However, it was not just their "low" students who faltered on the state tests. Students who had been identified as reading at or above grade level also performed quite poorly. As she looked again at the disappointing numbers, Principal Lansdowne couldn't help but wrestle with the idea that Rosa Parks Elementary was being set up to fail by the accountability system. Almost half of its students were eligible for free or reduced-price lunch and she was enrolling a growing number of immigrant students every year, many with very limited English skills. It seemed unfair that the school was held responsible for the results of students who had barely spent a year at the school, or for students whose lives were so difficult it was impressive that they even managed to make it through the day. Yet Principal Lansdowne worried that, despite the children's personal hardships at any given time, they would end up unprepared for life in the real world if they could not reach proficiency on a standardized test. She often told her teachers, "Mastery is mastery. If a child knows how to ride a bike, he should be able to ride when it is raining, or when he has a cold, or when he is on an unfamiliar road. The same is true of reading."

The Climate of Assessment

On many levels, the scenario at Rosa Parks Elementary is one that's emerging in thousands of schools throughout developed countries—the changing demographics of the population, assessments to monitor student progress, and systems to discuss student data, all as part of an (mandatory) accountability system driven by student assessment. And the outcome at Rosa Parks Elementary—disappointing results on the standards-based assessment—is also a common result. We are at a time when unprecedented amounts of data are gathered on children's skills and achievement, especially around literacy and especially in elementary schools. While collecting information on student performance is intended to cast light on instructional needs, all too often data are collected and scores are recorded for compliance reasons without actually benefiting teachers or students. To be sure, test results can be confusing, even discouraging; teachers, families, and students can lose sight of the possibility of improvement and success when repeatedly faced with low scores.

In order to promote their students' reading achievement, the looming and daunting challenge for educators is to ensure they have a comprehensive assessment approach that includes action steps to link assessment results to the day-to-day instruction in classrooms. This challenge is critical for schools like Rosa Parks Elementary because literacy assessments, when properly used and understood, can be the difference between a child receiving the help he or she needs or continuing to struggle as a reader. Assessment data can also be the difference between a classroom receiving standard, generic reading instruction or a curriculum modified to suit the specific strengths and weaknesses of the particular group of students. When implemented effectively, literacy assessments can in fact *reduce* anxiety and uncertainty for schools, teachers, and students. For example, they can guide lesson planning for a whole class, as well as inform a strategic plan of intervention for those who need extra help. It is possible to use literacy assessments to make better schools, better teachers, and better readers. The goal of this book is to lead the way.

A New Relationship with Data

In this book, we embark on a journey toward a new relationship with student data, as a means of promoting literacy achievement through instructional practice. Addressing the key challenge of establishing strong links between literacy assessments—including those collected for accountability purposes—and classroom practice is a critical next step toward school and student improvement in the field today. We bring to this challenge our lens as researchers who began our careers as an educational psychologist and teacher, respectively. Our work is focused primarily on literacy development, particularly for children from culturally and linguistically diverse backgrounds. We have spent many years working with schools like Rosa Parks Elementary, and even more time focused on individual students who struggle with reading, all while wrestling with issues of technique and the analysis of assessment results. We understand that instructional time is a precious, limited resource, particularly for a teacher with many students who face difficulties in reading; all time spent assessing students is time that is funneled away from teaching. We understand that the goal of reading instruction is not to produce a particular score, but to promote a love of text and a strong foundation in using print to learn and communicate. We also know that effective reading instruction is not easily accomplished. Good instruction is the result of professional expertise and planning, nearly always with limited resources. It would be impossible for publishers to create a program that is suited to the specific needs of your learners, so data are needed as the guidepost for creating a learning environment that is student centered.

In a new relationship with data, it is not enough to simply determine whether a child is "proficient" (i.e., at grade level) in reading. In elementary schools, and especially in the early grades, we also need assessments to give us indicators of potential risk before hidden weaknesses manifest as reading problems (Dickinson & Tabors, 2001; Snow, Burns, & Griffin, 1998; Scarborough, 2002). For those who are struggling, we need assessments to provide us with diagnostic information—that is, reasons why the students are struggling. In sum, we need to craft a developmental approach to assessment: a system to monitor students in key subskills of reading in order to identify risks, follow progress over time, and identify breakdowns when they occur.

A developmental approach to assessment is the foundation for genuinely differentiated instruction (Connor, 2011; Fuchs & Fuchs, 2005; Lipson & Wixson, 2003). In fact, a guiding principle of this book is that different assessments serve different functions. From a developmental perspective—one that focuses on the child—the purposes of assessment range from screening to progress monitoring to diagnosis (Sattler, 2008; Thorndike & Thorndike-Christ, 2009). From an accountability perspective—one that focuses on a group or system or institution—the purpose of assessment is primarily to assess performance against a set of standards, expectations, or benchmarks (Boudett, City, & Murnane, 2005). However, there is no single best test or assessment strategy. Rather, we need to put our efforts into selecting multiple measures and interpreting their results in appropriate ways to promote student success. It is how assessments are used—and with whom and how the results are interpreted and applied—that can be positive or negative, accurate or inaccurate. When used in accurate and ethical ways, nearly any assessment can help us learn about our students as readers and inform our instructional approach (McKenna & Stahl, 2009). For that reason, and given today's climate, as shown in Figure 1.1, we are better served to integrate the accountability and developmental perspective than to focus on a particular assessment approach.

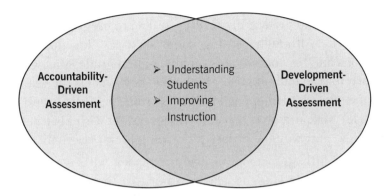

FIGURE 1.1. Integrating assessment approaches.

Therefore, instead of focusing on any particular test, or a particular skill, our goal is to build, interpret, and plan action steps around a comprehensive literacy assessment battery. The idea is to efficiently uncover students' needs, then to use that information to adapt and differentiate curricula and teaching with the systems and resources already in place, whenever possible. What we offer here is a process that can be used by any educator concerned with student reading performance—whether a district leader, principal, literacy specialist, or teacher—to build a comprehensive literacy assessment battery, interpret scores, and then connect to best practices for instruction.

Meet Our Rosa Parks Elementary Profile Students

In order to understand the intersection of the developmental and accountability perspectives, and how we might make strong links between the two in the name of informing instruction, we introduce you to four students at Rosa Parks Elementary whom we will discuss in subsequent chapters. They are presented in the order they appear in the book:

- **Carter** is a fourth grader who reads aloud with fluency and ease. He had been considered a good reader until he scored in the lowest category of performance on the state test at the end of third grade. While his teachers from the primary grades describe him as an eager participant, in fourth grade he is seen to be disengaged with novel study. His grades on story test are low, even though he is reading texts that are within his level according to assessments. Carter has become increasingly disruptive during class, and shows little motivation to participate.

- **Max** is a second grader; his reading skills are progressing but are below grade level. Although gaining some accuracy, his decoding remains laborious and his comprehension low. In first grade, Max was very eager to learn to read and interact with books; however, as the year went on he became much less interested in literacy time. Reading is now a source of stress for Max and he is constantly negotiating with his teacher, reading specialist, and parents for less time doing literacy activities.

- **Marcia**, a fifth grader, is an average reader with good fluency. Marcia is a Hispanic student who was born in the United States and has been enrolled in the same district since kindergarten; she is no longer designated as an ELL. Marcia is doing a poor job with (1) homework assignments, (2) answering text-based questions, and (3) participating in content-based discussions in the classroom. Her teacher knows that Marcia loves writing and generating stories—they are often displayed in the classroom—and he doesn't think that Marcia's performance of late is related to lack of effort or motivation.

- **Kim** is a first grader who learned to read before kindergarten and is the most advanced reader in her cohort. In her classroom, the majority of her peers are at, or slightly below grade level. In her spare time, Kim reads chapter book series, such as *Captain Underpants* and *Amber Brown*. During reading class, Kim gets frustrated and bored, sometimes blurting out answers, other times withdrawing and not participating. She has developed a reputation for being "bossy," and spends lunch and recess alone. At home she frequently asks to stay home from school, claiming that it's boring and easy.

These four students demonstrate complex needs, and each poses a unique challenge to his or her teacher. We will examine each more closely: Carter in Chapter 2, Max in Chapter 4, Marcia in Chapter 5, and Kim in Chapter 6. Then, in Chapter 7 we revisit each student in the context of a data-driven instructional model at Rosa Parks Elementary. Even as we explore these individuals, it is important to remember that it is not possible for most general education teachers to create a unique program for all of their students. Moreover, evidence suggests that robust instruction tends to benefit all students (Snow & Juel, 2005). In order to balance meeting the needs of individual students like Carter, Max, Marcia, and Kim with the demands of an entire classroom of students with profiles like those at Rosa Parks Elementary, we suggest, backed by strong evidence, a tiered approach to instruction.

A Tiered Approach to (Differentiated) Instruction: Starting with the Core

Modifying materials to make them accessible to our diverse group of learners is often referred to as "differentiation." True differentiation, however, is not a one-shot deal that is accomplished in a center or via an assignment, nor should it be relegated to educators affiliated with our Special Education or English as a Second Language (ESL) departments. Instead, we must find ways across the school and across the school day to make learning work for our students. In so doing, we want to ask ourselves if our assessment system, processes for understanding student data, and instructional practices are serving the greatest possible percentage of our students in the regular classroom.

Within a tiered instructional model—often referred to as response to intervention (RTI)—students participate in assessments on an ongoing basis and these data are used to inform instructional design and delivery (Fuchs, Mock, Morgan, & Young, 2003; National Center on Response to Intervention, n.d.; Lipson & Wixson, 2010). The model is particularly valuable because when implemented effectively daily instruction is strengthened, and students whose assessment results show risk receive supplemental, targeted instruction to improve their skills. Frequent follow-up assessments are used to monitor their progress; following up with students informs appropriate adjustments (or "midcourse corrections") to the intensity and approach of the intervention. Ultimately, this process also identifies students with special needs or learning disabilities, because these students often do not show improvement even when given the best possible instruction for their needs. In describing the use of this RTI model at scale, we focus on first using data to identify and understand the needs of the collective over the individual. Only once a strong and well-targeted *instructional core* (often referred to as Tier 1) is in place, can we begin to build interventions that will serve as truly supplemental and supportive instruction.

In our work with schools like Rosa Parks Elementary, we have found that it is common for specific classrooms or an entire school to display distinct patterns of strength and weakness, just as individual students have their own relatively strong and weak skills. After all, children do not grow up in isolation, but as part of families living in specific neighborhoods and communities. Research shows that cultural and linguistic groups often cluster in certain neighborhoods and schools (Orfield & Lee, 2005), and there are common child-rearing practices that influence the skills that children bring with them to preschool or kindergarten (Dickinson & Tabors, 2001; Hart & Risley, 1995;

Raikes et al., 2006). There are also certain practices and programs in place at schools that often highlight some skills over others, also resulting in specific strengths and weaknesses. The implication for schools, like Rosa Parks Elementary, is that even the best program of instruction will need to be adapted to suit the student population.

For these reasons, in our approach to data-driven literacy instruction using a tiered model, we focus on the collective before the individual. By accounting for collective, as well as individual needs, we can craft truly responsive instruction. The much less preferable alternative is relying on stand-alone tutoring sessions or supplemental programs as the strategies to catch up our low students.

When the RTI, or tiered, model is implemented well, there are two important positive consequences:

1. Assessment is closely linked to instruction across tiers. That is, assessment data informs decisions about daily instructional content and supports (*instructional core*, or *Tier 1*), to identify those learners who are in need of intensive interventions, and to further determine which students continue to struggle in the face of supplemental supports and are in need of further assessment and intervention to address their significant difficulties.

2. An emphasis is placed on *school contexts* and the quality of instruction. The focus is not just on individual children in need of targeted instruction, but on the appropriateness of instruction for meeting students' needs. This creates opportunities for conversations about school-level prevention models to meet the needs of diverse populations of learners. This is especially important for schools with high numbers of students from diverse linguistic and cultural backgrounds. Given the strong, three-way link between linguistic and cultural diversity, appropriate opportunities to learn, and student success, applying a tiered model shows real potential for designing tailored and effective learning environments.

Snapshot: The Practical Value of Starting with the Instructional Core

Have you ever looked at the results of an assessment and felt completely overwhelmed by students' needs? This has certainly happened to us, as well as to many of the teachers and schools we've worked with. One year, Sky was teaching third grade at a school on the brink of being penalized by the state, if not closed, for low assessment scores. As she looked at her class list of 21 students at the beginning of the year, only two were considered "proficient" readers according to the state test they had taken in the spring of second grade. Creating targeted intervention for 19 students was beyond her capacity for planning and not realistic within the time limitations of the school day. (After all, there are other subject areas that require time, instruction, and planning.) Not knowing where to start or what to do, she spent the rest of the year triaging her efforts from student to student, exhausting herself but never feeling as though she was really meeting their needs. Despite the best intentions, Sky did not have a clear strategy, and the result was instruction that was fragmented rather than cohesive. In the model we describe, assessments are used initially to identify the needs of the overall group of students. Thus, the first step is tweaking the *instructional core*, rather than planning small-group or individual lessons. If you are a teacher, this will include all the students in your classroom; if you are an instructional leader or literacy coach, or even an ESL specialist, this will begin with the entire school population. Only after systematic changes to the instructional core, and only when students' difficulties are clearly individual difficulties rather than a classroomwide issue, do we move to supplemental, targeted supports.

In Sky's case, this approach to tiered instruction would have helped her to make sure that the reading lessons were targeted to meet students' needs. No matter what, they would have received direct instruction that was learner focused, rather than guided by a teacher's manual or the latest professional development session. After all, a guiding assumption of this model is that with a strong and effective instructional core, no more than 20% of students should need specialized intervention. If you or your school has a larger number of students identified at risk, you are best served to first put significant time, attention, and energy into the instructional core.

Setting Off on the Journey

Assessment is the cornerstone of the RTI (or tiered) instruction model because it is through ongoing assessment that we are able to identify students' needs. Sometimes students' needs are obvious, but in many situations these needs can be hidden during the normal interactions of school and would be difficult to uncover without assessments (further discussed in subsequent chapters).

As a reminder, assessment scores do not represent the end goal of reading, merely a tool in the lifelong process of becoming a reader. That is, we do not teach reading so that a child can demonstrate a specific level of fluency, or be considered "proficient" on a state test, or even to do well on a college entrance exam. We want our students to love reading, to enjoy the private time spent alone with books, and then to be able to interact with others around the ideas they find embedded in the pages. At its best, reading connects us to a deeper understanding of ourselves and our possibilities—even helps us to improve our lives—yet we also need the skills to approach printed words with a critical eye.

However, the challenge of helping children develop strong literacy skills is complex and organic. Every year, every group and each student brings special reading challenges. While it would likely be impossible to craft an individualized approach for every one of our students, we can create learner-centered instruction by beginning with the collective, then accounting for the specific needs of certain students.

This book is organized into three parts. In Part I, we discuss all that is needed to make certain we truly understand our students as readers (see Chapter 2). This means crafting a comprehensive literacy assessment battery that will not only help us understand where our students' currently stand, but also the risks they might face as they encounter increasingly difficult, academically oriented texts throughout their schooling. Specifically, we explore in depth *how* to create and/or modify a literacy assessment system that provides valid information useful for planning appropriate instruction for the population of interest. A fundamental basis for this plan is balancing the needs of the group with the needs of struggling students (see Chapter 3). Do not worry—this system is not meant to be about an increase in testing; rather it is about ensuring the system in place is comprehensive and capitalizes on information at hand, all the while minimizing redundant sources of information. After all, we, as authors, have each worked in settings where *too much* assessment data are collected.

In Part II, we discuss how to interpret and analyze the results in order to identify instructional needs and effectively monitor progress for special populations. This includes students who are struggling (see Chapter 4) and ELLs (see Chapter 5).

The third and final section of the book is about action steps: how to take the information identified from assessments and apply them to instruction. This does not involve scrapping the current program, or throwing the teacher's edition of the core curriculum out the window. It involves thinking carefully about how time is allocated within the literacy block, and what areas are prioritized for instruction. This can be accomplished within our current curricula and programs; indeed, even textbook publishers encourage schools and teachers to use materials as a foundation that should be modified for particular students. Here, we begin by understanding how to shape the general practices and instructional routines used with all students in a school or classroom (see Chapter 6), and how these can be better adapted to meet specific needs. We then conclude with two chapters: one focused on the nuts and bolts of school-wide models of data-driven instruction—what systems absolutely need to be in place at the school level (see Chapter 7), and one focused on the challenges, key steps, and rewards of effectively leading schoolwide change to improve reading achievement (see Chapter 8).

In the words of Lao-Tzu, "The journey of a thousand miles begins with a single step." The next step is to turn to Chapter 2, where we begin by discussing the many different skills that go into what we call "literacy," and how we can begin to understand our students, such as Carter, Max, Marcia, and Kim, both collectively within their school population and individually as readers.

Why Many Readers Fail

It was a typical morning in Franny Bartek's fourth-grade classroom. She sat at the kidney-shaped table with one of her reading groups while around the room students were either reading alone, working in centers, or meeting with their novel study groups, chairs pulled into circles. As her reading group took turns reading paragraphs, she looked up and scanned the room. Amid the low hum of voices, the students seemed engaged and on task. From all appearances, Carter was hard at work, too: he sat at his desk, hunched over a text, eyes moving as he looked over the page. It would have been necessary to stand beside him to see the magazine cradled between his hands and the inner lip of the desk. Meanwhile, his copy of *Charlotte's Web*—the text he was supposed to be reading during class—sat abandoned on its cracked spine.

This had become typical behavior for Carter, who managed plenty of minor distractions during reading class—talking with friends, passing notes, even rolling his eyes and refusing to answer questions. The behaviors were mild, so Franny wasn't as concerned with discipline as she was with what appeared to be a new, less engaged relationship with school. Her own children were now in middle school, heightening her awareness of how dramatically children can change during this transitional period. Before this year, Carter had been a star student, with the polite manners and strong work ethic that made his teachers and his mother proud. His success was particularly endearing because his father had left home when he was in kindergarten; the 5-year-old Carter was incredibly quiet and shy in kindergarten, struggling to regulate his emotions and make friends. Despite these early setbacks, there was something about his dimpled smile that made him a staff favorite, and by the middle of first grade he was reading better than many other children in his class. By third grade he was able to read passages at a rate associated with proficient fifth graders. He was a Rosa Parks Elementary success story, with the confidence and popularity to match.

Carter's early achievements in reading, however, did include one major red flag. His third-grade state test score put him in the "warning," or lowest, category for reading. As Carter started fourth grade, it seemed as if this low score actually foreshadowed problems to come, rather than being the fluke result of an off day, as school staff had previously believed. As well as he did with basals and anthologies in the primary grades, he was bored with the novels he was assigned for book study as a fourth grader. Within a few months the misbehaviors began and his grades dropped. Even so, he was still measuring above grade level on the diagnostic assessment Rosa Parks Elementary uses to identify students' reading levels. His pacing and expression were a little off, but he read through the words quickly and smoothly, with the confidence of a student who feels good about his ability to read. When his teacher called home to see if something was amiss, Carter's mother made it clear that everything was fine at home, although Carter now complained chronically about having to go to school.

What was going on with Carter? Perhaps the greatest challenge in understanding students' literacy development has to do with the complexity of successful reading. Literacy is a multifaceted construct, requiring the coordination of a whole set of skills and abilities for success. Even when given a simple passage, a student must understand the relationship between letters and sounds and then decode the words with sufficient automaticity and fluency to have enough cognitive "space" left over to simultaneously process the narrative. At the same time, the child must understand the meaning of most of the words and have some ideas about the structure of the passage in order to comprehend. And, of course, the student must be engaged in the reading task, understanding the purpose for reading that passage or book, and be motivated to participate. There can be a breakdown at any point in the process, and often the breakdowns are not visible.

Stemming from the multidimensional nature of reading is a counterintuitive aspect of reading development: A student may be at risk for reading difficulties, yet not struggle visibly with text or be well below grade level. That is, in the absence of assessment, students may appear to progress in reading, particularly in the primary grades, yet still have specific weaknesses that can cause problems down the road. Carter is a prime example. When Franny volunteered to try out some additional assessments for Rosa Parks Elementary with her students, it became clear from the results that despite Carter's impressive fluency, his vocabulary knowledge was quite limited and his reading comprehension was shaky. In fact, he had one of the lower scores in his class in vocabulary—an outcome that took his teacher completely off guard, especially since he was a good conversationalist with a clever sense of humor. The emerging picture of Carter was one of a student who was able to decode words, yet did not always understand the meanings of what are often termed *academic* words; that is, words outside our sight-word lists and decodable readers and everyday conversations, but frequently found in written texts. While this did not pose much of a problem in the primary grades because of the relatively straightforward nature of the simple storybooks Carter most often encountered, by fourth grade it made it very difficult for him to understand, much less enjoy, the novels he was assigned, filled as they were with advanced words and even figurative language. His challenges were reflected in the poor grades he received on quizzes given after every chapter, and also explained his difficulty on the standardized exam. Misbehaviors began as reading came to represent an interminable list of words and abstract concepts rather than exciting stories full of interesting characters and, more often than not, predictability.

Like many students in schools today, Carter was experiencing the difficulties sometimes associated with the "fourth-grade slump," yet he was not necessarily "failing" or performing well-below average. Although he doesn't stand out as a poor reader in class, he is at high risk for declining academic performance with every advance in grade level. He is an example of why we need comprehensive assessments in place to monitor progress across grade levels and ensure our students are learning and growing across various aspects of literacy. If different assessments had been used, Carter's academic vulnerabilities—and those of many children like him—might have been recognized much earlier, long before he began to struggle with the meaning of novels. Indeed, with appropriate assessment and data-driven instruction, his fourth-grade problems might have been completely avoided.

Uncovering Students' Needs

When we work with schools like Rosa Parks Elementary, we nearly always observe that certain types of literacy skills—those related to making meaning of texts—are consistently left out of assessment batteries used to identify which students need additional instructional support. In early literacy batteries, meaning-based measures are a gaping hole. Given this assessment gap, we are not surprised by research showing that these same areas are often left out of daily instruction, sometimes despite the teacher's best intentions to teach these literacy skills (Baumann, Kame'enui, & Ash, 2003). We often talk about the importance of providing a balanced approach to reading instruction; similarly, it does not make sense to measure performance in just one area of reading and use that score to build an entire reading program or intervention for a struggling student. Such an imbalance would make it far too easy for assessment scores to tip instructional balance, with the skills that are measured receiving priority for instructional time, planning, and professional development. Another common but undesirable outcome of an unbalanced approach is that students like Carter fall through the cracks.

Balance is particularly crucial when serving students who might be considered "at risk." In any school where instruction is provided in English, we expect a percentage of students (usually no more than 10%) will struggle significantly and persistently with "cracking the code"—that is, learning to read words—regardless of socioeconomic status or ethnicity. However, decoding is only one part of successful reading that is demonstrated by strong comprehension of grade-level texts of various genres. Indeed, research has found that decoding is not the greatest challenge for many students, especially for the growing population of those from culturally and linguistically diverse backgrounds (August & Shanahan, 2006).

This brings us to the complexity of reading comprehension, which is multifaceted in nature. Many skills go into what we call "comprehension"; the act of meaning making while reading is a dynamic process for all of us. Our own reading comprehension—and that of our students—involves interactions among at least three different factors: (1) our set of skills and our knowledge base as a reader, (2) the text we are engaged with, and (3) the purpose of the reading activity itself under any given circumstance (Cartwright, 2008; Duke, Pressley, & Hilden, 2004; Gaskins, Satlow, & Pressley, 2007; RAND Reading Study Group, 2002). At the level of the reader, comprehension difficulties may be due to a number of factors, including but not limited to inaccurate and/or inefficient word reading, underdeveloped vocabulary knowledge, and oral language. With respect to vocabulary and oral language, there are several dimensions to this knowledge, including understanding the meanings of individual words, the way they fit together syntactically, and how they fit into the text as a whole. The reader might also lack relevant prior knowledge, or may possess that knowledge but fail to activate it; to learn while reading, a reader must actively build upon his or her background knowledge by integrating new learning with prior understandings (Anderson, 2004; Kintsch & Kintsch, 2005). As other potential sources of comprehension weakness, the reader might fail to deploy effective meaning-making strategies while reading, or might lack the understanding of the purpose for reading in that context. As mentioned, it is often the interaction of some of these factors—in combination with the text at hand—that ultimately influences the comprehension process (Alexander & Jetton, 2000; Anderson, 2004; Bransford, 2004; Kintsch & Kintsch, 2005).

Pushing on the complexity of the comprehension process, it is also worth noting some of the key characteristics of any given text that influence meaning making: the nature of the language used by the author, including the sentence structure; the words themselves, which are often more rare and specialized than those we use in everyday speech; the way information is organized on the page and presented (we've all seen textbook pages with so many different text boxes and marginal notes, it's hard to know where to focus); and the extent to which the author might use literary tools to convey information such as similes, metaphors, and analogies.

Because reading comprehension is multifaceted in nature, as students progress from the primary grades into the more complex reading demands of upper elementary school and onward, problems with reading comprehension often emerge even for students who decode automatically and are fluent readers (Biancarosa & Snow, 2006; Chall & Jacobs, 2003). This was the case with Carter. Typically these difficulties stem from skills related to children's language development and their background and conceptual knowledge—what it is they are learning about the world. Nonetheless, it is still possible to screen for these weaknesses that cause reading difficulties and adjust instruction accordingly. We need to be sure that our assessment systems catch up to this important finding in the field.

In this chapter, we address a critical assessment issue: schools and teachers can only uncover students' needs in the areas that are being measured. As shown in Figure 2.1, in an effort to start to organize ourselves to understand

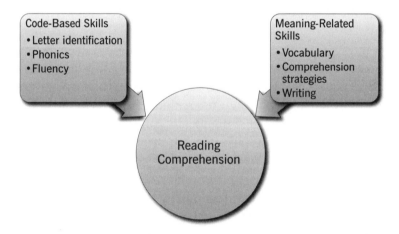

FIGURE 2.1. A broad look at reading comprehension.

this complex process we call reading, we focus specifically on two broad categories of difficulty: code-based and meaning-related skills. While it is impossible to systematically measure every aspect of reading that may lead to difficulties, we cannot afford to have a blind spot as large as one of these broad areas. Both *must* be represented in the assessment battery for data-driven instruction to prevent reading difficulties and ultimately school failure. Keep in mind that the specific skills being measured within each category will depend upon students' ages and the resources of a school or district. Let us now discuss each category in turn.

Code-Based Skills

Code-based skills are those that allow students to read words, or decode, with accuracy and efficiency. The way in which these skills are taught and measured change from year to year in elementary school, with diminishing attention over time as skills become established. A kindergarten teacher will likely focus on very basic elements of decoding, such as hearing sounds in words, identifying letters, and matching letters with their sounds. By first grade, students are learning to sound out words with increasingly complex letter–sound relationships, as well as building up a solid repertoire of sight words (i.e., words that are immediately recognized and read without decoding). By the time a student is in second or third grade, the focus is often on reading with the appropriate pacing and accuracy, as well as understanding multisyllabic words. All along the way students are expected to read more quickly and accurately if they are going to perform at grade level (Hasbrouck & Tindal, 2006). For more on the development of word-level skills, we recommend *Words Their Way* (Bear, Invernizzi, Templeton, & Johnston, 2011).

One defining characteristic of code-based skills is that they are discrete, with a very specific and clear end goal. For example, there are 26 letters in the English alphabet. While they can appear in upper-case and lower-case forms, as well as in various fonts, the task of knowing letters is constrained. The limited universe of letters, and even their sound correspondences and combinations, means that mastery can be accomplished. Similarly, research has shown that a first grader who can read a never-before-seen passage at the rate of at least 40 words correct per minute (WCPM) by the end of the year very likely has a strong foundation in word reading (Good, Simmons, Kame'enui, Kaminski, & Wallin, 2002). Forty WCPM is a clear benchmark for all first graders, and one that hopefully all of our students can attain.

The discrete nature of code-based skills makes them relatively easy to measure. While any testing situation introduces some ambiguity (e.g., the child seemed to know the letter *E* in class; did he miss it on the test because he was tired or did not understand directions? Or has he not mastered the letter *E*?), code-based skills are fairly straightforward to measure. Improvements can be clearly demonstrated and are easy to document and celebrate. As a result of this discrete nature, there are many assessments to measure code-based skills and they are generally popular among both publishers and educators. Table 2.1 shows some of the ways that code-based skills are measured by grade level. Take a moment to think about the code-based skills measured at your school or district.

TABLE 2.1. Common Measures of Code-Based Skills

Domain	Description	Common measurement techniques
Phonological awareness	Phonemic awareness (PA) is the most commonly assessed aspect of phonological awareness skills. It is the ability to *hear* sounds in words, an important skill for eventually connecting letters to sounds. Typically, PA is not measured past first grade, except in the case of individual struggling readers.	• Rhyming (sometimes thought of as a separate piece of phonological awareness). • Identifying initial sounds. • Manipulating sounds in words. *Example*: using colored blocks (one color per sound), changing /m/ /a/ /p/ (*map*) to /t/ /a/ /p/ (*tap*); child then changes the first block with a different colored one. • Producing the sounds a child hears in a word (e.g., /m/ /a/ /p/ for *map*). *Example*: Teacher says, "Here is a picture of a goat, a car, and a hat. Point to the one that starts with the /h/ sound."
Phonics	Phonics is the ability to *match* letters to sounds. For beginning readers this can mean identifying the sound a letter makes; for more advanced readers this can involve decoding complex letter–sound combinations like *steigh* (a non-word).	• Identifying letter sounds. • Reading out loud a series of non-words. *Example*: Teacher says, "Read the following: *tup* *zag* *thig*."
Fluency	Fluency is the ability to read accurately, efficiently, and with prosody (the appropriate pacing and expression), although very few assessments measure prosody.	• Accuracy: the percentage of words a student reads correctly in a passage. • Rate: the number of words a student reads correctly per minute (or another time increment) in a passage or a list of words.

Meaning-Related Skills

seperate + distinct *— double meaning* *greater extent/quantity*

Meaning-related skills are far more ambiguous than code-based skills. Whereas code-based skills are discrete, meaning-related skills can be vast, even infinite. There is not nearly the same clear progression of development of these skills over time, to be easily assessed, as there is with code-based skills. Meaning-related skills involve the repertoire of strategies, coupled with the background knowledge of the words, text, and topic required to understand what is being read. Most meaning-related skills fundamentally involve language comprehension, which is shaped from the moment a child is born. Perhaps the central language comprehension skill, and perhaps most amenable to assessment, is vocabulary. In order to make meaning from text, a child must have a good command of the meaning of the words that appear within it. For example, if we listened to Carter read *Charlotte's Web* aloud, we would note his ease in reading a simple word like *runt*, and perhaps even a harder word like *injustice* smoothly. Yet, if he does not understand what these words mean, he will have difficulty understanding how or why the character Fern convinced her father to spare Wilbur, the small weakling piglet of the litter. Imagine all of the words you would expect a student like Carter to understand as a fourth grader, not to mention words like *web* that have multiple meanings depending upon the context in which they are used. Indeed, most school-age children should understand tens of thousands of words, acquiring 2,000 to 3,000 words per year. The student graduating high school needs to have good command of about 50,000 words (Stahl & Nagy, 2006).

Given this complexity and the size of the problem spaces (e.g., as compared to our 26 letters) it is not surprising that meaning-related skills are not only tricky to measure systematically but also to gauge informally. Very often, the way in which we're teaching reading and the materials we're selecting in the primary grades mean that the demands of the vocabulary in reading assignments keep pace with the level of skill needed to read these words until third or fourth grade. Moreover, there are some students whose code-related skills are so limited that it is difficult to ascertain whether problems in understanding text originate in decoding or language comprehension—or both. Max, another Rosa Parks Elementary profile student whom we introduced in Chapter 1 and will further discuss in Chapters 4 and 7, is an example of a student whose code-related difficulties impede the development of his meaning-related skills. Max could only read words far below his grade level; for Max, these texts placed minimal demands on his vocabulary knowledge and comprehension skills.

Catching up in meaning-related skills is a difficult task, particularly when years of schooling pass before problems are identified; this is why we need to adjust the way in which we're assessing and teaching reading in the primary grades. To understand fully, let's look back at Carter as a kindergartener. When tested at school entry, Carter knew about eight upper-case letters and a handful of lower-case letters. Any kindergarten teacher will recognize that Carter did not have a strong foundation in early code-based literacy skills before entering school. Vocabulary, however, was not part of Rosa Parks Elementary's early literacy screening system in kindergarten; although a teacher might recognize on his or her own that Carter did not know many letters, how would he or she be able to tell that the shy little boy did not have a strong vocabulary? The problem of vocabulary gaps is not small. Research shows that children like Carter may know about 4,000 fewer words than classmates with high vocabularies by the time they reach second grade (Biemiller & Slonim, 2001). In little more than a year after entering kindergarten, Carter was able to catch up with his peers in identifying letters, connecting them with sounds, and hearing the sounds in words, due in no small part to the dedication and expertise of his kindergarten teacher. However, catching up in his word knowledge when he was potentially thousands of words behind is from the outset a far greater job, and in Carter's case, a job the teacher didn't formally know that she had.

Again, it is important to understand that being at risk in meaning-related skills does not mean that reading difficulties are unavoidable or entrenched. What it does mean is that students like Carter, and many of his peers, require a more deliberate approach to teaching vocabulary and comprehension. As discussed in Chapter 1, this instruction should be part of a tiered system: as important as intervention can be for students like Carter, he also needs direct, explicit instruction in vocabulary as part of the instructional core. These efforts at the level of the instructional core (Tier 1) can be supplemented with targeted interventions (additional tiers of instruction) for students who show individual difficulties with vocabulary. Unfortunately, because his teacher did not know that Carter (or any of his classmates) had vocabulary weaknesses, she did not structure lesson plans in such a way as to focus on vocabulary and word knowledge, a process we discuss in depth in Chapters 6 and 7. While she certainly went over the word lists in the curriculum used by the school, there was no overarching emphasis on building language through conversations, sociodramatic play, and books. It was far more obvious and compelling, given the assessment battery being used by Rosa Parks Elementary, that Carter and many of his classmates needed help identifying letters. His teacher invested much time teaching letters, even creating special letter cards for Carter to take home to practice. While it is important to explicitly teach code-based skills (National Institute of Child Health and Human Development [NICHD],

2000), they can receive undue attention and focus. And because assessment was unbalanced, instruction was too. For more on comprehension and vocabulary development and instruction, we recommend *Reading Instruction That Works* (Pressley, 2006) and *Bringing Words to Life* (Beck, McKeown, & Kucan, 2002).

What do you know about your students' meaning-related skills? Generally, it takes a specialized task to uncover risks for meaning-related skills, the type of task that would only be part of an assessment battery. Table 2.2 highlights methods for measuring meaning-related skills. As you look at the table, think of whether and how you are including meaning-related skills in the literacy assessment battery.

TABLE 2.2. Common Measures of Meaning-Related Skills

Domain	Description	Common measurement techniques
Vocabulary	A child's vocabulary includes the words that are familiar to him or her. In promoting reading, the general goal is to promote both breadth and depth of vocabulary. For any given word, there are differing levels of knowledge, such that a child may fall anywhere on a continuum of the word sounding familiar to being able to use the word flexibly, even metaphorically, and creatively in both reading and writing. The number of words a child knows is often vast, so words included in assessments are often meant to represent a class or type of word, rather than to serve as an inventory of words a child must know.	• Receptive/listening vocabulary: The child indicates he or she understands a word he or she hears by pointing to a representation of the word. • Expressive/speaking vocabulary: The child is asked to produce a word after being shown a picture or given a definition. • Definitions: The child is asked to identify which option gives the best definition (e.g., "In the sentence, which option most closely fits the definition of *brush*?"), or asked to produce his or her own definition (oral or written).

Comprehension	Comprehension requires a child to connect with the meaning of a passage that he or she has either heard (listening comprehension) or read (reading comprehension). Reading comprehension is more commonly measured after first grade; listening comprehension beforehand.	• Multiple-choice questions:
		  ○ Information questions ("Where did Tony find the treasure?")
		  ○ Inferential questions ("Why did Tony stomp out of the room?")
		• Short-answer or open-answer questions: "What would you do if you saw Jamaica in the playground with your toy?"

Interpreting Results from Meaning-Based Assessment

In theory, the issue we are raising in this chapter sounds simple: measure students' code-based and meaning-related skills in order to drive instruction that meets the full range of their needs. However, the reality is a bit more complex. Imagine that Carter is a first grader, and his teacher has just looked at results that flagged Carter on a vocabulary measure. Because we care deeply about our students, these types of results are often frustrating. From her perspective, the teacher knows that Carter is a great child: smart, funny, and hardworking. He reads well and participates fully in classroom discussions. It may feel as if the assessment is ignoring his strengths or perhaps is just wrong. The words used in the assessment may seem too difficult or inappropriate, as if they pose an unfair expectation for a child like Carter, given the context in which he grew up. (We all have a favorite story of an item on a vocabulary test that seemed impossible for a student to know—Sky's favorite example from teaching in rural New Mexico was *subway*.) After all, Carter is not struggling. His vocabulary is more than good enough for him to communicate effectively at school and at home.

Indeed, there is nothing *wrong* with Carter. Vocabulary differences occur because children receive different amounts and types of exposure to language from their very first days on earth. How would Carter know a word like *runt*, for example? A child who lives on a farm or who participates in picking out a new puppy or kitten may be familiar with the idea of a "runt" from conversations around his experiences. A preschooler might learn the word from a storybook read to him or her at bedtime. In general, small and subtle differences in the everyday routines of children influence vocabulary levels. Some children consistently hear fewer words, and the differences begin to add up. Even the types of words a child hears at a dinnertime conversation has an effect on his or her vocabulary level (Dickinson & Tabors, 2001). Little children who regularly hear storybooks often develop a broad range of vocabulary because of the wide range of words and topics featured even in simple picture books. Research shows us that children who are asked to talk about memories, feelings, and make-believe topics build language skills more quickly than those asked to label pictures or talk about what they presently see and hear (Dickinson & Tabors, 2001). While these differences generally do not impact the way that children interact in their day-to-day lives, they can have real consequences when they need to read, and particularly when faced with academic texts.

Just as surely as there is nothing wrong with Carter, there is nothing wrong with the assessment. Despite what may seem like odd word choices or unusual procedures that lack context, measures of meaning-related skills signal important instructional needs. As we point out in Chapter 1, it is the way in which the score is interpreted and used that makes an assessment good or bad, useful or potentially harmful. For Carter, a bright child with many strengths, his vocabulary levels put him at risk for future reading difficulties because the vocabulary demands of participating in academic settings are very different from the vocabulary demands of participating in normal social life. However, his vocabulary will build as he receives repeated exposure to new words over time and would definitely be accelerated if he were immersed in a rigorous language-learning environment. Likely Carter has other peers who need increased instruction in vocabulary, so his teacher's first step should *not* be to create an intervention program for him, but to thoroughly analyze the way that vocabulary is taught in the core of instruction. Even if the test happened to underestimate his vocabulary, there is no harm in implementing better vocabulary instruction. As we discuss in Chapter 8, good vocabulary teaching is a far cry from going over a list of words and assigning definitions; instead, good vocabulary teaching—best done as part of a schoolwide effort and thus discussed when we outline leading such change—builds knowledge, critical thinking, reading comprehension, and even writing skills. Unfortunately, the inverse possibility that Carter actually needs more vocabulary work, yet this need is overlooked or dismissed, is harmful.

The Fluency–Comprehension Disconnect

Having the opportunity to work with schools like Rosa Parks Elementary over many years, we have seen far too many students who perform well on code-based measures, yet not nearly as well on meaning-related measures. These are students who perform at low rates on reading comprehension measures and who struggle with reading difficulties in the upper elementary and middle school years. These are also students whose difficulties are likely to persist and ultimately impede their academic success in significant ways.

In Figure 2.2, containing findings from Nonie's research, we show a striking example of a word reading–word knowledge disconnect for a sample of U.S.-born children of Spanish-speaking immigrants who attended preschool as 3- and 4-year-olds (students like Marcia, one of our four profile students) and who were followed through middle school. Figure 2.2 shows that at age 11, after many years of classroom-based instruction in English, their word-reading skills are at the level expected for their age (50th percentile), while their vocabulary knowledge (a proxy for background knowledge and oral language skills) is well below average (20th percentile). What's very important in the context of

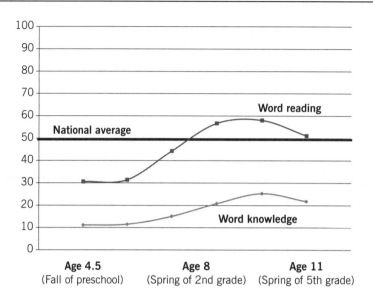

FIGURE 2.2. The word reading–word knowledge gap.

this book and work is that, on average, these students would have performed well on an early literacy battery that targeted code-based skills. Other research by Nonie and her team suggests this reader profile is much more common than we might have thought—not just for our language-minority learners who come to school not fully proficient in the language of instruction (Lesaux, Kieffer, Faller, & Kelley, 2010) but also for many of their English-only classmates, especially those from low-income families (Lesaux & Kieffer, 2010). We want to be sure that our assessments will identify this profile long before we face a scenario like Carter's.

Restoring the Balance

A major goal of a solid, comprehensive literacy assessment battery is to understand the development of our students' literacy skills over time. As we discussed earlier, in order to have a more complete picture of how our students are currently performing and to gauge their risk of later reading difficulties, it is imperative to include measures of both code-related and meaning-related skills. In this chapter, we have focused primarily on meaning-related skills. The focus is not meant to imply that code-related skills are unimportant, either to measure or to teach. There is clear and compelling evidence that direct instruction in code-related skills is best practice for preventing word-reading difficulties (for relevant reviews see Snow et al., 1998; NICHD, 2000). Our argument is that while code-related skills are necessary for students to reach their reading potential, they are not sufficient. Strong word reading is not necessarily a gateway to good comprehension; it is a necessary but not sufficient relationship. Meaning-related skills are more likely to be left out of assessment batteries, simply because they are a bit harder to measure and interpret and perhaps because they take more time. However, increasing focus on meaning-related skills will help students for the long term, particularly our students from linguistically, culturally, and economically diverse backgrounds. Moreover, these

HOW VOCABULARY KNOWLEDGE DEVELOPS: A TALE OF TWO BEES

It was a hot and sunny summer day. A couple sat at a table in a family-owned restaurant, eating their lunch, while a kamikaze bee repeatedly flew into the window, buzzing loudly as it looked for an escape. From the next table over, a small boy, fascinated by the buzzing bee, came over. He extended a sticky finger, pointed, and said, "Look! A fly!"

How would you expect his parents to react? Some parents would see the moment as an opportunity for a science lesson. They would likely discuss why the insect was a bee, not a fly, perhaps talking about anatomy or the yellow and black stripes of a bee. They might ask the child to remember a time he was stung, or talk about the importance of bees for pollinating plants.

A different child in the same situation may face a completely contrary reaction. The parents may see the interaction as a learning opportunity of another sort, reprimanding the boy for interrupting the couple's lunch, and pulling him away. Any discussion of the incident would probably focus on why it is rude to approach strangers.

Neither response is right or wrong, but reflects different parenting goals. Nonetheless, either scenario, if representative of a general pattern of parent–child interactions, will probably shape the child's behavior and instructional needs at school. Imagine the same child now a few years older, sitting at the rug during story time in kindergarten while the teacher reads a Big Book on bees. In the first scenario, the child may better understand the story because he has already talked about bees and learned about their characteristics at home. Then again, he may be more likely to interrupt his classmates as they try to share their own answers and stories. In the second scenario, the student might not understand the story unless the teacher points out the meaning of some words while reading, or spends time interacting with students around words with multiple or complex meanings. Either way, the teacher will need to adapt the lesson to meet the student's needs in regard to his background knowledge.

skills are just as critical in kindergarten and even prekindergarten as they are in fourth grade and beyond.

Measuring Across Domains

Take a moment to fill in Form 2.1 (at the end of the chapter), which has you consider the assessments in use in your school or district and whether they measure code-based or meaning-related skills. If a single assessment has many subtests, you may wish to fill in one row per subtest in order to get a complete picture.

What are the gaps in your assessment battery? In what grade or skill areas would you need additional assessments in order to gain complete information on your students as readers? Once you have an idea of the areas that are being measured you will be ready to put together a comprehensive assessment battery, the goal of Chapter 3.

FORM 2.1
Assessment Inventory

Assessment	Code Related or Meaning Related?	Specific Skill(s) Measured

An Assessment Battery That Works

The leadership team at Rosa Parks Elementary had convened in the school's conference room for an early meeting on assessments. The requisite box of doughnuts was placed in the center of the table and each team member entered armed with a big mug of tea or coffee. Indeed, as the morning progressed, the caffeine felt particularly necessary despite the relatively small agenda. The meeting had begun easily enough, with fourth-grade teacher Franny Bartek presenting her student Carter as a case study. The team then discussed how his instructional needs came into focus once specific domains of literacy were measured (see Chapter 2). For the remainder of the meeting Principal Lansdowne had planned a group task to build on this discussion. The team would inventory the school's current literacy assessment battery in order to identify gaps in two ways: the domains of literacy captured by the current assessments and the type of information being gathered. As we discuss below, it was this second goal—understanding the type of information being gathered—that was a challenge for the group.

On the conference room walls Principal Lansdowne had hung several pieces of chart paper listing each literacy test given by grade level, with a blank column for the team to write what skills their current assessments measured. However, charting the assessments gave rise to a conversation that had its share of confusion and disagreement, particularly around the properties of the assessment they administered every fall and spring to determine students' reading levels. The assessment, described in Chapter 1, requires each student to read passages that are progressively more difficult to determine the level he or she could read at an independent or instructional level; that is, a passage the student could read with at least 95% accuracy, as well as correctly answer questions on the content.

Although the teachers at Rosa Parks Elementary had used the test for years, they were not entirely in agreement on what the assessment measured. "The test is definitely measuring comprehension," one teacher argued. "That is why there are questions after every passage. It's checking for understanding." The reading coordinator at the school was not convinced. "How can it measure their actual comprehension skills when the questions are on the students' reading level, rather than on grade level?" she asked, also pointing out that the test was more accurately a measure of code-based skills because teachers calculated the percentage of words that students read accurately, a measure of fluency. "Plus, let's be honest here," she pressed. "How hard are those questions anyway? Do they really get at a deep understanding of the passage? And what kinds of passages are used? We have plenty of students like Carter, who appear to be on grade level, yet who are not proficient on standardized tests."

Franny nodded her head in agreement. Carter, after all, had done fine on the few simple questions included in that particular assessment. He had done well enough that his identified reading level surpassed the point Rosa Parks Elementary had specified, with guidance from the district, as the desired goal for the beginning of fourth grade. "I hate to see us bash this test because, to me, this assessment is really useful. But not for the reason we are talking about," piped in a veteran fifth-grade teacher. "I am using it to match readers with books they can understand and make my reading groups. I guess I'm confused because I don't see a column for that." Principal Lansdowne spoke up at this point. "I think we need to push ourselves to be clear on the purpose of our assessments. If we are going to invest the time and resources into testing all of our students, we need to be more comprehensive. So while it is great to have an assessment to help us group our students for tomorrow's reading lesson, I don't think it's enough to meet our larger student improvement goals."

Aligning Assessments with Their Purpose

There is much confusion about the intended and appropriate use of assessments in the field of reading instruction today, particularly as test publishers try to align their products with the demands of the educational market. For example, at Rosa Parks Elementary one very broad instrument was used to identify those students at risk and also measure students' reading performance over time. Among staff there was clearly some confusion about its value and purpose. To be sure, the assessment was not designed to serve the multiple purposes Rosa Parks Elementary had attached to it. School staff would need to take action in order to identify their assessment needs—as related to instruction and intervention—and align these needs with appropriate testing tools.

As we identify purposes for assessment, we often realize the promise of data-driven instruction. After all, a strong literacy assessment battery does far more than identify whether a child is reading on grade level; it can identify weaknesses that may result in difficulties, or identify where breakdowns occur. It might also tell us about strengths and weaknesses across groups of students—by grade level, or by skill. In every school, there needs to be a system in place for the general student body that would flag a student like Carter, ideally before he or she shows significant reading difficulties and weaknesses in reading-related skills, and then have assessments in place to monitor his or her progress as instructional adjustments are made to meet the student's needs. This system should also support daily instructional planning.

RTI, discussed in Chapter 1, is a framework for doing just this—integrating assessment information with an instructional approach intended to prevent reading difficulties and provide timely supports for those who may struggle. While this model means different things to different people, assessment is the cornerstone of the model; at its core, assessments are used to uncover students' instructional needs, adjust the reading block, and support intensified instruction for those identified at risk (Fuchs et al., 2003; National Center on Response to Intervention, n.d.; Lipson & Wixson, 2010). In order to determine the overall efficacy of our instruction and identify those students at risk, we must cast a wide net over the school (or classroom population), gathering information on code-based and meaning-related skills, using different types of assessments.

Using the Right Tools

As mentioned, observing development in code-based as well as meaning-related skills in an effort to give a complete picture of reading development is an important component of the assessment process (discussed in Chapter 2). But this is just a starting point for establishing a high-quality reading assessment battery. Moving beyond the domains of literacy, within a comprehensive literacy assessment battery different *types* of testing tools are needed, with each tool serving a clear and specific purpose. By including different types of measures, some of them formal and some informal, we gain an overall sense of a child's performance but also hone in on specific skills that may be placing a child at risk for reading difficulties (McKenna & Stahl, 2009). This level of information can be critical for the classroom, driving instruction in a way that will help children thrive as readers. Within the RTI model, tools that make up a comprehensive assessment battery together serve important and distinct functions in the service of student improvement. These four types of tools include:

- **Diagnostic:** Testing to inform instructional groupings, lesson planning, and targeted instruction.
- **Screening:** Testing to identify whether students are at risk in a particular literacy domain; that is, whether they hit an established benchmark for proficiency.
- **Progress monitoring:** Testing over time—that is, multiple data points with the same measure—in order to gauge growth or a learning trajectory.
- **Outcome:** To gauge achievement at the population level in order to determine the effectiveness of an educational program.

There is no hierarchy to the types of assessment tools. Each is as important as the next to understanding student performance and development, and in fact, every type is needed for an effective, comprehensive assessment system to drive tiered instruction and school improvement (Hosp, Hosp, & Howell, 2007). Yet, as we discuss in this chapter, schools are more likely to have some types of assessments than others. And while it is not uncommon for marketers to claim that *one* test can provide multiple types of information, in reality, the design of most tests limits how effectively than can serve more than one purpose (for discussion on these issues see Koretz, 2008). To clear up any confusion around the types of assessments, each is described in detail below and summarized in Table 3.1.

In taking a developmental approach to literacy we recognize that literacy skills are dynamic and are expected to grow rapidly over the elementary years. There is no clear point demarcating when a student goes from being at risk to having a difficulty, or as discussed in Chapter 4, to having a profile that resembles that of a student with an identified disability. Therefore, diagnostic, screening, progress monitoring, and outcome assessments are interrelated, and we will best understand students when we integrate multiple sources of information (Hosp et al., 2007; McKenna & Stahl, 2009). The end goal is an assessment battery that identifies student risk in clear, teachable domains so that we can, accordingly, adjust instruction and then monitor students' progress in relation to our adjustments.

TABLE 3.1. Assessment Types and Purposes

Type	Description	Who participates
Diagnostic	Diagnostic assessments help us to understand student performance in authentic context, particularly to inform immediate lesson planning and intervention. They may be informal (e.g., teacher observation) or formal (e.g., commercial battery). They are the assessments most closely aligned with instruction.	All students participate in ongoing diagnostic assessment for instructional purposes. Students with specialized needs often require more formal diagnostic measures to better understand their needs (see Chapter 4).
Screening	Screening assessments provide a clear indicator of whether students are "at risk" in specific domains of literacy. In order to do their job, they must have an external benchmark or norm that has been carefully validated through test development to demonstrate where students perform relative to peers across the nation. All screening measures are formal. Often, they are relatively brief.	All students participate in some screening assessment. However, additional screening windows may be built in for students who were flagged as being "at risk," to follow up on their progress and potential reclassification.
Progress monitoring	Progress monitoring assessments are used to gauge student growth over time, as compared to a trajectory that has been carefully validated through test development. All progress monitoring measures are formal.	Students who demonstrate individual risk. The specified window ranges, but is often somewhere between every 3 to 6 weeks.
Outcome	These are standardized tests that provide information on the success of an overall program and/or school based on student achievement levels in broad areas. These are the farthest removed from everyday instruction. All outcome measures are formal.	All students participate in outcome measures, usually as mandated by an accountability system. While exceptions may be made for certain populations of students, including those with severe disabilities or very limited proficiency in English, many students with special needs participate in these assessments with the support of testing accommodations.

Diagnostic Instruments: Daily Nutrition and Exercise

In elementary classrooms, diagnostic assessments should be as common as alphabet strips and backpacks. Like the critical role that daily nutrition and exercise play in one's health over the long term, diagnostics sustain good teaching practices by informing instructional groupings and lesson planning, across the day and across school years. Whether asking questions to check for understanding, performing a running record, or giving a unit or story test, teachers are regularly undertaking diagnostic assessments to inform their instructional groups. These assessments are driven largely by having a child perform a regular classroom task with the goal of understanding, with the help of a rubric or scoring framework, the student's level of mastery. Some diagnostic assessments are formal—they come in kits and require training and individual administration in a quiet space. Examples include the Developmental Reading Assessment (DRA, Beaver, 2006), Fountas and Pinnell's Benchmark Assessment (Fountas & Pinnell, 2007a, 2007b), and the Observation Survey (Clay, 1993). Others are part of a packaged literacy curriculum and might be used with the whole class, such as a test or quiz students take after reading a book or chapter. Still others emerge from a teacher asking questions and taking notes with the support of a rubric or observation checklist during a lesson.

Certain key features of diagnostic assessments distinguish them from the three other categories of assessment (i.e., screening, progress monitoring, and outcomes). First, we think of these assessments as taking place largely "in meaningful, authentic contexts" as the behavior asked of a child during a formative assessment is very similar to what he or she might do on any given school day (if it is, in fact, separate from a lesson). Most commonly this entails reading a passage at or near a student's independent reading level and answering questions—the same way Carter was assessed as part of the assessment battery used at Rosa Parks Elementary. Second, the results are immediately useful to the teacher in planning his or her approach to instruction. They let him or her know what level of readers to assign to a child. Through the process used to measure student performance a teacher can often determine whether a child needs, for example, extra practice with any given skill, such as their knowledge of the suffix *ed*.

There is, however, a third distinguishing characteristic of diagnostic assessments: they do not include an established or formal external benchmark against which to interpret the results. This is always the case, even though schools and districts, and sometimes test publishers often set goals or guidelines for each grade level. For this reason, diagnostic assessments used day-to-day most often provide only a sense of student strengths and weaknesses relative to classmates. Although sometimes such instruments are marketed by publishers as able to serve progress-monitoring purposes, they have not been through the rigorous testing needed to ensure that they measure growth over time against an established and validated growth trajectory. (To use the language of psychometricians, diagnostics are not "technically adequate" to follow growth.) This is a subtle but important difference; it can be thought of as the difference between marking off a child's height on a growth chart year-to-year versus the growth chart a doctor uses. The chart in the doctor's office has been developed to compare height against a growth curve calculated from analyzing thousands and thousands of children and therefore includes parameters that let us know, with a good deal of certainty, when a child is at risk. The one at home, on the other hand, only tells us, for example, that the child is growing and by how much each year—a relative rather than absolute assessment (for more on this see McKenna & Stahl, 2009).

If we think back to the case of Carter, we arrive at this cautionary tale about diagnostic instruments: their results were not meant to be interpreted outside of the classroom and teaching context. When there isn't a clearly estab-lished "outside benchmark" to which the reader is compared, we may not, for several years, know how our readers are doing outside of our school buildings because school populations within a district can vary in their achievement levels. At a school like Rosa Parks Elementary, where a large percentage of stu-dents are at risk for reading difficulties, a child may look strong compared to his or her peers yet not be fully on track to becoming a strong reader.

Because these assessments are closely tied to daily instruction, they are crucial for the work of teachers and crucial for a comprehensive assessment system; they are like the daily nutrition and exercise that goes into the recipe

WHAT ABOUT DIAGNOSTIC ASSESSMENTS AS PART OF FORMAL EVALUATION?

When students have significant, persistent problems in the face of significant and varied educational supports, specialized assessments are required to bet-ter understand the sources of difficulties and create a personalized intervention plan. Chapter 4 discusses struggling readers in depth, including considerations for diagnostic assessments. There, we discuss the fact that formal evaluation for special education services should only come about following persistent, pro-longed difficulties *and* targeted intervention efforts.

for good health. They should, in fact, be what we spend the most time on and should be seen as a very useful teaching tool to help with the design of tomorrow's lesson. So if teachers are not using their results and don't feel the test is valuable, it is not a worthwhile exercise. If such measures are in place and are not driving targeted instruction, leaders should reconsider the system and tools, aiming to find something that feels more useful for teachers and/or ask themselves whether sufficient professional development has been provided to make the tool and information useful for teachers. There is no other use for data from diagnostics; because of their technical properties and local purpose (to inform instruction), they should *not* be submitted for accountability purposes. As discussed further below, there are many other instruments that are much more technically adequate for that job.

Screening Instruments: The Routine Checkup

In the world of reading assessments, a screener is like an instrument used at a checkup at the doctor's office. These assessments are a level removed from day-to-day classroom instruction and provide a reference for performance outside the curricular context—they measure a child's performance against a set norm or benchmark that has been carefully established by the developers, based on analyzing the results of hundreds (even thousands) of children. Screening assessments can provide clear information about student risks relative to the expectations for the specific age or grade level in clearly defined skill areas (i.e., code-based and meaning-related skills), much like the growth chart at the doctor's office gives a clear sense of a child's height and weight compared with other children the same age. Examples of screening assessments include the Dynamic Indicators of Basic Early Literacy Skills (DIBELS), the Gates–MacGinitie Reading Test (MacGinitie, MacGinitie, Maria, & Dreyer (2000), the Peabody Picture Vocabulary Test (PPVT; Dunn & Dunn, 1997) and the Test of Word Reading Efficiency (TOWRE; Torgesen, Wagner, & Rashotte, 1999).

Just as the checkup is in the office, with instruments like a blood pressure cuff, thermometer, and stethoscope, the actual tasks asked of a child during the screening assessment are decontextualized and different than day-to-day activities to maintain good health. For example, the test may be timed or the child may be asked to read through passages that are above his or her reading level. Or, perhaps the child is asked to read a list of non-words, when in the classroom the teacher may have stressed the importance of connecting words to meanings and has not expressly taught students to read non-words. The implications for instruction are less intuitive than those tied to diagnostics because the tasks are not part of regular classroom instruction; like a checkup the measures signal a potential problem, but it is up to the doctor to dig further into any issues that surface and then prescribe a treatment. So in the same way that taking a child's temperature is an indicator to be compared to a norm (98.6°F), a score on a screening assessment can provide a clear indication of a problem. If a child has a fever, though, it could be for all kinds of reasons; taking the child's temperature doesn't necessarily identify what is making the child sick or what steps are needed to alleviate the illness. Screening assessments, then, lay the groundwork for identifying the source of a problem (see Part II of this book) and a corresponding treatment (see Part III) by signaling that a child is at risk and merits further attention. In sum, screening assessments in reading give clear indication of risk in specific domains through set benchmarks or criteria, or by telling us how a child performs relative to peers of the same age or grade level. Moreover, these tests often tell us about risks that may not be apparent from classroom interactions alone, such as whether a child has enough vocabulary skills to understand the passage he or she decodes.

Because the scoring process involves comparison to a set norm or benchmark, these assessments are particularly useful for understanding performance

WHAT DO I NEED TO KNOW ABOUT NORM- AND CRITERION-REFERENCED ASSESSMENTS?

When we conduct screening, progress monitoring, and outcome assessments we want to understand how a student's performance stacks up against expectations for that grade or age level. There are two ways we can make these comparisons: through norm-referenced or criterion-referenced assessments. *Norm-referenced* means that performance is compared against what is observed for the population of children at that age. For example, a growth chart plots a child's weight against the range of what is typical for that age resulting in different types of scores including a percentile rank. That is, we know whether a child is at the 15th, 50th, or 85th percentile for weight compared to same-age peers. In contrast, *criterion-referenced* means that performance is compared against a set benchmark (usually called a "cut score") that has been established through careful testing and analysis. Rather than focusing on ranking the individual's performance, these results can be likened to a "pass" or "fail" test—they tell us strictly whether the child hit the expected level for skills or knowledge, providing us with no other information. As mentioned in the doctor's office, for example, 98.6°F is the established criterion for a normal temperature. Despite their differences, both norm- and criterion-referenced assessments work well for establishing student risk.

across groups of students. By aggregating scores it becomes possible to know whether a weakness (or strength) in a particular skill is a district phenomenon, school phenomenon, classroom phenomenon, or a phenomenon at the level of the individual student. Many experienced teachers are expert at identifying the needs of their students, but it is difficult to hold a mental picture of the development of 20 (or often more) children in various skill areas that go into literacy outcomes—skills that are developing at different rates. It also doesn't help inform how the school's students are doing, overall. Assessment scores make this information concrete and visible. They also provide insight into how our children will perform when they need to read in contexts beyond the realm of the classroom and (perhaps) in the absence of a familiar teacher. Finally, understanding risk helps with planning instruction broadly—more on this in Chapters 7 and 8.

Progress Monitoring: The Follow-Up Appointments

At our checkup in the doctor's office when something seems amiss such as our blood pressure level, the doctor generally does some follow-up assessment immediately, generating a hypothesis about what might be the right course of treatment. And if we leave with a prescription, whether for exercise and a modified diet or a specific drug, we also return to the doctor's office much sooner than we would have without the red flag. As soon as we're back in the office a few weeks later, the doctor will first assess blood pressure—to find out if there is still cause for concern and whether the course of treatment decided on at the last appointment is, in fact, the right strategy. If blood pressure is lower, then we might "stay the course" in terms of treatment; if not, the doctor will revisit the treatment plan, making a "midcourse correction." In this way, our progress monitoring assessments are closely tied to our screening assessments; in fact, sometimes we can use the same tool for both purposes. The key is that the tool always compares the observed level or score against an outside benchmark that reflects the expected level.

It is easy to see how this analogy relates to the school setting; when we have a student whose performance on a screening instrument raises a red flag, we undertake further assessment—using our diagnostic tools described above—and then decide on the right course of treatment. The student's subsequent performance is assessed on a regular basis (e.g., weekly, monthly). Progress toward meeting the student's goals is measured by comparing expected and actual rates of learning, and then instruction is adjusted as necessary. Those who struggle may need additional observation points. As discussed in

Chapter 4, this would include a more specific and nuanced examination of student work and frequent progress monitoring. And for our overall population we want to be sure that we have some idea that the treatment plan—our daily reading instruction—is supporting their growth as readers, in all domains of literacy. It is only through ongoing progress monitoring assessment that we are able to identify students' needs and ensure our readers' levels of mastery. There are at least four key purposes of progress monitoring assessment:

- Determine whether students are benefiting appropriately from an instructional program.
- Identify students who are not demonstrating adequate progress.
- Build more effective instructional programs for students who are not benefiting.
- Compare the efficacy of different forms of instruction and use this comparison to design more effective, individualized instructional programs.

For a list of progress monitoring assessment options, visit the National Center on Response to Intervention website, *www.rti4success.org*, and click on *Tools and Interventions*.

In our work with schools and in our academic research, we find there is both an art and a science to progress monitoring. While we certainly need specified benchmarks to best understand our students' trajectories, we also need careful observation to fully understand our students in context. Therefore, progress monitoring is most effective when it is an instructional *mindset* rather than just a set of assessments. In a sense we're always playing the role of detective, being careful not to take a one-size-fits-all approach to our instruction. Note, too, how different the assessment tool and the treatment are—they are not related. It is through further assessment, professional judgment, and relationships that allow us to know the child as an individual that we best implement intervention. Sometimes the adjustments we make will need to address motivation and interest as much as specific literacy skills.

Outcome Assessments: Stepping on the Scale

Outcome assessments are those formal assessments typically given once or perhaps twice annually. In today's climate of assessment-based accountability, outcome assessments in elementary schools are usually standardized or standards-based tests mandated by a government body in order to measure annual progress. The main purpose of outcome assessments it to provide an indication of the overall achievement levels of the test taker in a given domain. Just as body mass index produces categories (e.g., normal weight, overweight), outcome test results are often used to categorize students (and in turn schools) as "warning," "in need of improvement," "proficient," or "advanced." Because these assessments are designed to understand achievement levels in broad academic areas, they provide the least detailed information to drive daily instruction of the three types of assessments. They are the "farthest" from daily instruction, but they are also the results that are perhaps the most informative for school, district, and state leaders who are focused on school improvement, literacy rates, and the results of reform efforts. Their results can tell us about the extent to which a school's reading program is meeting students' needs, or if certain groups appear to be responding better than others. For this reason, results are often disaggregated by race, free/reduced-price lunch status, and disability status, and used as a measure of equity. At the end of the school year outcome assessments provide information on how the larger school and/ or district community performed toward their long-term goals for student achievement.

Different Assessments for Different Purposes at Rosa Parks Elementary

With these four purposes and tools for assessment, let's return to the leveling assessment used at Rosa Parks Elementary, the subject of discussion at the meeting led by Principal Lansdowne, which we discussed at the outset of this chapter. Although it was a formal assessment administered individually to each child, the testing procedure—reading passages and answering the teacher's follow-up questions—is, by nature, a diagnostic assessment. It involved a teacher and a child engaged in a task that is very similar to regular instruction, and scoring was driven by teacher observation of the student performing the task with the support of a rubric. To be sure, as the fifth-grade teacher pointed out, the results will help teachers at Rosa Parks Elementary form their reading groups for daily instruction and match students to texts for independent reading. Although the scores on this measure can be very useful for understanding students' text needs during small-group guided reading, they do not provide information about how a child will confront a passage or book once removed from the supportive environment—whether taking a standardized test or at home reading a novel at grade level. Therefore, as was shown by Carter, whose score was above reading level on the assessment, the test was not able to identify which students were at risk for reading difficulties in either code-based or meaning-related skills. And for other students who are already clearly struggling, such as Max (whom we hear more about in Chapter 4), it doesn't help the teacher distinguish what is at the core of the problem without a deeper investigative strategy, as would be signaled by low scores on a screening measure.

By this leveling measure, a diagnostic measure, many students at Rosa Parks Elementary were quite successful at reading in their classrooms. Almost all students showed growth on the assessment from fall to spring. In contrast, the annually administered state test (outcome assessment) evaluated the overall performance of the school's student population against a set benchmark at one point in time, and in this case, deemed the school not meeting annual progress. This scenario was both alarming and discouraging for staff, for many reasons. Most significantly, they were caught unaware: The state test did not match the otherwise optimistic picture they had of their students' performance and growth because they had not included benchmarking assessments that would have provided a clear indication of how their students stacked up relative to national performance levels on literacy skills.

Rosa Parks Elementary is not alone. Many elementary schools have assessment systems in place that include strong diagnostic assessment practices and, by mandate, outcome assessments beginning around third grade. These schools work very hard to get to know their students in the domain of literacy development, from kindergarten (or even prekindergarten) until they leave for middle school. They establish schoolwide goals, develop plans, and create units of study, all with the goal of getting their students to reach reading proficiency. However, many are missing the crucial link between diagnostic and outcome assessments—screeners and assessments to monitor progress to gauge student performance against outside benchmarks over time. Screening and progress monitoring assessments, which provide clear indicators of student performance relative to all students at that age level in a specific skill area, are a very reliable gauge of whether the student is on level or at risk in any given area of literacy. They provide useful information for teachers then to probe deeper, using diagnostics, and to ultimately inform targeted instruction, but also to the school and district leaders seeking to understand their population as readers, and to support teachers through professional development programs. By strategically incorporating screening and progress monitoring measures into their assessment system a teacher, school, or district can create a comprehensive literacy assessment battery that will reliably identify students at risk and promote a mindset of tailoring instruction to meet their readers' needs, supporting strugglers through targeted intervention and regularly undertaking midcourse corrections, long before Carter and his peers are anchored in middle childhood and faced with a standardized test that is much too difficult.

In an ideal scenario, assessment efforts would be coordinated into a cohesive, vertically aligned assessment battery across a district or school—we lay out such an approach in Chapter 7. However, it is certainly possible for individual teachers to build their own literacy battery that responds to the issues brought up in this chapter. Within her own classroom, Franny Bartek narrowed in on her own approach before Rosa Parks Elementary formalized a plan, partnering with her colleagues teaching fourth grade. First Franny identified key areas she wanted to assess in fourth grade: the code-based skills of phonics and fluency, and the meaning-related skills of vocabulary and reading comprehension. The idea was for the assessments to help her identify students like Carter, who might appear to be fine yet still face risk in terms of reading, while helping her understand better why some of her other students struggled in reading. Some tests could be used broadly with all of her students to screen for potential difficulties; meanwhile, she would frequently monitor student progress through careful observation of individual work and the informal assessments included in her curriculum. Franny knew that her job would be to follow up particularly closely, maybe even with different measures and more frequently, with students who were flagged by the screening assessment.

Identifying the Types of Assessments Used in Your School

Now is the time to look at your current assessment system with a critical eye. Schools need to create a cohesive literacy assessment system that makes sense across grade levels. Teachers need to consider the type of information they have on their classroom of students. Complete Form 3.1 (at the end of the chapter) to document the properties of the assessments being used at your school. If a single assessment has many subtests, you may wish to fill in one row per subtest in order to get a complete picture.

While all four types of tools—diagnostic, screening, progress monitoring, and outcome—and their respective purposes are important to understanding the instructional needs of students, most schools only have pieces of a comprehensive battery. When an assessment battery is, indeed, comprehensive, you will notice that:

- Both code-based and meaning-related skills are measured at regular intervals.
- It includes a combination of diagnostic, screening, progress monitoring, and outcome assessments to provide information on student risk and progress.

With a comprehensive literacy battery in place, ideally aligned across grade levels, you will have a strong foundation to interpret scores and understand sources of difficulty (see Part II of this book), and then plan action steps for differentiating instruction (see Part III).

Assessment Inventory

	Assessment	Purpose	Literacy Skills Measured (code related, meaning related)
Diagnostic			
Screening			
Progress Monitoring			
Outcome			

Assessment Considerations for Special Populations

CHAPTER 4

Assessment to Support Struggling Readers

As soon as she had dropped off her students for dismissal, second-grade teacher Pam Perez walked straight back to her classroom, ready to shut the door and decompress. A winter wash of afternoon light streamed through the window, as if to emphasize the stillness of the room without her students. Out of habit she put a lone chair up on a desk and collected a few stray pencils for the "extras" cup she kept by the sharpener. She looked around the space she had so carefully arranged, from the standards and rubrics on the wall to the various centers and stations for student work to the books grouped into plastic baskets, spines labeled with the reading level.

For the first time that day she sat at her teacher's desk, capitalizing on an uninterrupted moment. Today she could not get Max off of her mind. He was a quiet, sweet boy who had a knack for drawing realistic racing cars that included the tiniest details, down to the rims and decals. He was also struggling to learn to read, a battle he had been fighting since kindergarten. This was Pam's fourth year of teaching and she felt determined to help Max become a better reader, a challenge she had initially felt confident she could tackle. She had put him in a small reading group with appropriately leveled text and made sure that he got extra instruction in phonics each day, either with her or with one of the school's volunteer tutors—a woman who was working with some of the students reading far below grade level. Today, however, she felt her confidence shaken.

It all started when Pam agreed to observe the tutor. In that particular lesson, the tutor had cut out letters that Max would put in front of the word family *in* to create a word. As the tutor placed new initial sounds, Max read: tin, pin, thin. When he reached the word *min*, Pam interrupted to ask, "Is that a real word?" They spent a few minutes discussing the issue, settling on the conclusion that *min* was not a real word but sounded almost like the (real) word *men*. Pam repeated the question for the next word that arose, *shin*. Max looked up at Pam, shaking his head. "Shin isn't a word," he said with a smile, turning back to the task at hand, ready for a new match. Pam was surprised, so she pressed the issue a little harder. "Wait a minute, Max. Isn't there a body part called a 'shin'?" Max looked back up, his head cocked to the side in a contemplative gesture. Finally he shook his head "no." "Well, what is this?" the teacher asked, lifting her knee up toward her chest and pointing to her shin. Max looked back at her with a timid expression—he knew by now that he was missing something—and answered "your leg?"

Pam could not help but worry this wasn't an isolated error—that Max was starting to learn to sound out words but without making sense of them. Max was a native English speaker, and *shin* seemed like such a basic word. And just the other day, when all of the other kids were laughing and giving examples during a discussion of the word *curmudgeon* based on a character they encountered during story time, it seemed to have gone over his head, as if the word were lost on him. But they had encountered and discussed it several other times in the last couple of months during story time. Were there other words that Max did not know? He had been able to answer story questions during small-group time, but Pam knew well that answering the comprehension questions with the simple decodable books assigned to the lowest group took little insight; in fact, she suspected many students would be able to answer the questions without even reading the text. Pam sighed, feeling overwhelmed by the task at hand. Max might need much more assistance than tutoring in phonics but Pam was not sure what this might entail, or where to start.

In this chapter we focus on using data to identify our readers' instructional needs, so we can best serve our students and use time most effectively. Speaking very generally, we know that some children will need help with code-based skills, some with meaning-related skills, and some with both. The rest of this chapter is devoted to getting us past the general and into the nitty-gritty. We will learn how to better understand the needs of individual students who are identified as at risk through the variety of assessments included in school, both progress monitoring and diagnostic in nature. The goal is to mine the data at hand to find rich information that can be directly linked to the tiers of instruction.

An important caveat to this work is that individuals can only be clearly identified as having risks when most of their peers are performing at grade-level expectations; otherwise, it is difficult to disentangle individual development from the instructional environment. Once the patterns in the data have been analyzed to determine whether risks are located within the classroom or school, individual students usually emerge who demonstrate risks that are not part of these overall patterns. These are students who will likely need support beyond the instructional core—and we need good data to determine what that should look like. An important purpose of the assessment battery is to better discriminate among these at-risk readers, and in turn, target instruction to their needs.

We follow the principle that an effective process is one that starts with the big picture, then narrows in on specific risks. As you read, you may find it helpful to keep in mind a specific student you know of or work with, and/or to think about Max, or even Carter and Marcia—our other Rosa Parks Elementary students who are struggling readers—and what information you might need to better design an intervention plan for him or her. Throughout the chapter we aim for efficiency, acknowledging that time is a precious, limited resource to be maximized. We know this is especially the case for a teacher like Pam, who often has several at-risk students she needs to find out more about, perhaps not all as severe as Max but nevertheless with a wide range of possible sources of their difficulties.

A Tiered Assessment Model to Support Struggling Readers

In the first section of this book we outlined a comprehensive screening and progress monitoring battery that would work for the entire school population. While such an assessment battery provides a good deal of important information, we often need more details to best support the instructional needs of struggling students. As we described in Chapter 1, progress monitoring assessments function like a thermometer. When a child has a temperature above 98.6°F, we know that the child has a fever but we do not necessarily know the cause. Just because a child is "at risk" in phonics does not mean we provide a generic code-based intervention. We need to know where the problem is located. In order to help all students, we provide different levels of assessments depending upon the student's needs. Thus, just as the effective instructional model is tiered, so too is the effective assessment model.

At Rosa Parks Elementary, teachers were particularly concerned with how data could be used to help struggling readers and to inform differentiated instruction. As shown in Figure 4.1, within a tiered assessment model all students participate in some testing. These tests help screen for difficulties, make sure students are on track, and also allow us to see how well our program is serving our students. If a student is not progressing as we would expect, additional assessments are needed—both to inform the design of our instructional support plan and to inform us as to whether these efforts are working. At the outset, we need to determine the student's current levels of performance and *specific* areas of weakness. In an RTI model, we also need to understand how a student responds to our intervention efforts; thus the need for frequent progress monitoring of struggling readers.

An important dimension to the effective assessment system—especially critical for identifying and supporting struggling readers—is that data are collected *over time*. That is, multiple, routine checkups and check-ins are built into the school year. Collecting data over time on individual students is the

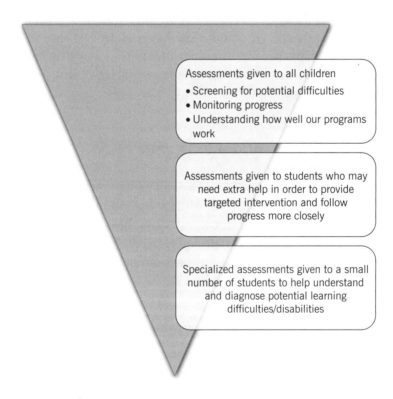

FIGURE 4.1. Assessment to support the RTI model.

only way we'll have informed answers to many of our most critical questions about supporting students. This is the case whether our questions are about what a student's likely RTI is, what performance levels we can expect from particular students with particular profiles, or whether the majority of our students overcome certain weaknesses. These data may be collected in the short term or over the longer term; during a 6-week intervention period or over the course of the academic year, for example. The critical issue is that we have *multiple* data points.

Why the emphasis on assessment *over time*? We know that if we are to prevent reading difficulties, we need to identify at-risk students in a timely manner, and in turn, provide appropriate, targeted intervention; therefore, *ongoing* assessment has to be commonplace. After all, reading development is a dynamic process. "Reading" at age 3 is not the same as reading for a 5-year-old, which is not the same as skilled reading for a 9-year-old, and none looks similar to skilled reading for a college sophomore (Chall, 1996). A reader's ability has to keep pace with the changing demands of the context and the purpose for reading but also in response to instruction. Therefore, it is ongoing assessment that should guide our program designs, classroom practices, intervention goals, and clinical services; importantly, it should do more than just tell us about the overall effect or outcome of any one practice, it should also inform our midcourse corrections and modifications.

Yet so often, the assessment data that is most frequently referenced in meetings about struggling readers focuses on a single point in time. Consequently, we get a "snapshot" of performance and describe it accordingly—we talk about a student whose performance is below grade level; we talk about the percentage of students whose scores are in the "needs improvement" range and figure out what strategy we're going to use with them; we even talk about a student's score and speculate that it may have declined. But there is so much we don't *really* know about that performance—whether for the population or the individual—as it relates to that child's development. That is because the data on which we're basing our judgments focuses on just one point in time.

Looking at Data to Design Supplemental Instruction

While each of our students is unique and individual, there are some common patterns of reading performance that emerge from assessment data. As a first step toward understanding the at-risk reader, consider whether the following three questions can be answered based on the available data:

1. Does the child read words with efficiency (i.e., exhibiting code-based skills) but display weaknesses in word knowledge and/or effective comprehension of passages (i.e., meaning-related skills)?

2. Does the child show difficulty with decoding (i.e., code-based skills) but show strong word knowledge and comprehension skills (i.e., meaning-related skills)?

3. Does the child show difficulty with code-based skills as well as meaning-related skills? If so, which skills specifically in each domain?

When considering a student who struggles with reading, you will likely answer yes to one of the three above questions. Each question is aligned with one of three common reading profiles—students with code-based risks, meaning-related risks, or some combination of the two. Considering these "buckets" gives an immediate sense of where we want to focus our energies and where we might conserve time. These profiles are particularly useful for shaping the literacy block for students. They also help us understand whether our students are displaying problems that are different from those of their peers.

Let's put Max's performance in the context of his classroom peers. Table 4.1 is a chart that shows the percentage of students in Ms. Perez's room that were identified as at risk on the fall benchmark assessment. The scores are displayed to show what is being measured—either code-based or meaning-related skills, then more specific skills within each category (phonics, fluency, vocabulary, and comprehension).

Given this information, let's think back to Max. When Ms. Perez looks up Max's latest test results (see Table 4.2), she confirms what today's exchange with the tutor suggested: His meaning-related vocabulary and comprehension skills are actually well below average. Compared to classroom results, Max's difficulties with vocabulary and phonics stand out, yet it also becomes clear that Max is one of many with fluency weaknesses.

TABLE 4.1. Percentage of At-Risk Students in Ms. Perez's Classroom

Literacy skills			
Code-based skills		Meaning-related skills	
Phonics	Fluency	Vocabulary	Comprehension
35%	63%	24%	45%

TABLE 4.2. Max's Risk Levels

Literacy skills			
Code-based skills		Meaning-related skills	
Phonics	Fluency	Vocabulary	Comprehension
High risk	High risk	High risk	High risk

These results remind us that we want to make sure that Max has opportunities through whole-class, small-group, and center work to promote both his code-based and meaning-related skills. Chapters 6 and 7 provide strategies for making sure that the overall instructional environment meets his needs, as well as the needs of his many classmates who are also experiencing difficulties with reading.

Of course, in real life, the skills that students display are far more complex and nuanced than the three broad instructional profiles outlined above. To be sure, the results from screening assessments are just a starting point for the at-risk reader. To plan intervention lessons and additional supports for Max requires much more detailed information. For example, at this point we have an idea that Max needs support in both code-based and meaning-related skills, and that supplemental instruction is needed in phonics and vocabulary specifically. However, that still leaves Ms. Perez with unanswered questions: What are Max's sources of difficulty with letter–sound combinations? How can he most effectively learn new vocabulary?

The next step is to use all the information at hand to fill in the details about a student's needs. Just as we want to save time and resources by focusing interventions to the specific needs of students, we also want to focus on

---

REFRESHER FROM CHAPTER 3: SCREENING ASSESSMENTS

Scores on screening assessments can tell us about a student's level of risk in a particular literacy domain. Criterion-referenced tests provide a cut score (or a "benchmark") that categorize students as being at risk, whereas norm-referenced scores let us know levels of risk by providing a percentile score or stanine that compares a student's performance to others of the same age or grade level. For example, children below the 21st percentile (in the 1st and 2nd stanine) are performing very poorly compared to their peers and against the national average; they are at high risk for academic difficulties in the domain the assessment measured.

the resources we have at hand to understand student performance. To narrow in on these specific needs, there are methods for using already administered assessments to learn more about our students as readers. This allows us to maximize the information already in hand and minimize the need for additional testing. In many ways, understanding the needs of at-risk readers is true detective work, hunting down details in assessment booklets, student work, and classroom interactions. So, let's look more closely at the data using a two-pronged investigative process—using screening and diagnostic data; an approach that reminds us that, in many cases, the whole is greater than the sum of the parts.

Investigative Strategy 1: Taking a Second Look at Progress Monitoring Measures

Many times, examining individual students' testing booklets and forms provide a wealth of information for understanding students' needs. For example, examining Max's test booklet (shown in Figure 4.2) actually proves very enlightening for planning intervention (for a resource on how to do this well, see *I've DIBEL'ed, Now What?* (Hall, 2006). Any given booklet might show, for example, whether a student had a low score because of errors, or whether the student had the knowledge but lacked automaticity to produce them quickly. For a student like Max, taking a careful look at a testing booklet can provide rich information. The teacher can identify which words were missed in

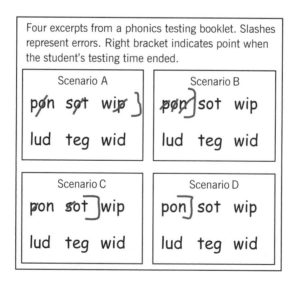

FIGURE 4.2. Sample test booklets.

a passage: decodable words or sight words. Even a simple list of consonant–vowel–consonant words can give information on students' struggles. Look at the four scenarios in Figure 4.2. What do you notice? Some very clear patterns emerge, each with its own set of instructional implications. In Scenario A, Max consistently missed the medial short vowel sounds—a very different situation from Scenario B where he missed nearly all letter sounds, Scenario C where he skipped the initial sounds, and even Scenario D, where he knew all the letter sounds but produced them too slowly.

Each of these scenarios immediately suggests a different focus for intervention. While some computerized test programs automatically produce instructional recommendations based on students' scores, it's of question whether the algorithms used do or do not account for these fine-grained patterns of performance. You will want to double-check test booklets before, for example, having Max practicing sounding out nonsense words. If Max's test booklet fits Scenario A, he may know his consonant letter sounds well and have no difficulties with initial and final sounds, so we wouldn't focus on those during his supplemental instruction. (Consider this: Would the tutoring scenario described in the beginning of this chapter be the best use of time in this case?)

As is so often the case in reading, gaining a deep understanding of meaning-related difficulties can be more challenging than analyzing code-based skills. As discussed in Chapter 2, there are many coordinated skills involved in reading comprehension, so it can be difficult to understand whether, for example, a child struggled with a passage because he or she did not have enough background knowledge, stamina to get through the text, or a combination of both. Yet, examining test booklets is also useful for meaning-related skills. Comprehension assessments may let you know whether a child missed literal questions or ones that require inference skills or understanding of word meanings. You may also be able to identify certain types of words that are missed in a vocabulary exam. Some test makers even provide grids that identify the types of speech or other categories for words in order to perform an error analysis.

Investigative Strategy 2: Using Diagnostic Assessments with Struggling Readers

In concert with screening assessments, diagnostic assessments are often particularly useful to understanding sources of difficulty and usually require minimal time away from instruction. Many of these may not be formal assessments; they may include the tests and assignments that are part of your curriculum, often administered to students after a story or a unit.

WHAT KINDS OF MEASURES TO MONITOR STRUGGLING READERS?

To be sure we are tracking struggling students' progress over time and adjusting our instruction as needed, we need to have the right kinds of measures to do so. They need to be sensitive to small changes in growth and zero in on particular skills that are targeted by instruction and intervention. Often the measures that allow us to do this well are curriculum-based probes and/or other more informal measures.

Data based on diagnostic assessments provide the added benefit of context to better understand the scenario and an opportunity to better understand how students perform in a more natural setting, which may require a broader range of skills. For example, many common screening assessments for phonics ask children to read a list of consonant–vowel–consonant non-words. But in everyday texts children encounter a far more varied and complex range of spelling–sound combinations (e.g., *sleigh*). When Pam administered a running record, a diagnostic assessment that involves marking errors made by a student when reading a passage, she immediately noticed a pattern. Max often skips word endings—simply leaving them off—even though he was recently taught common suffixes and he appears able to read word endings correctly in isolation. It's clear that by attending to learning in context, Pam can refine and increase the precision of her classroom-based support plan.

It is clear that screening and diagnostic assessments complement one another and strengthen our overall instructional approach. In this scenario,

---

RESOURCES TO SUPPORT DIAGNOSTIC ASSESSMENT AND TEACHING

Among the many books out there to support teachers in their quest to better understand and serve struggling readers, three are very widely used:

Howell, K., & Nolet, V. (1999). *Curriculum-based evaluation: Teaching and decision making* (3rd ed.). Florence, KY: Wadsworth.

Kibby, M. W. (1995). *Practical steps for informing literacy instruction: A diagnostic decision-making model.* Newark, DE: International Reading Association.

McKenna, M., & Stahl, K. (2009). *Assessment for reading instruction.* New York: Guilford Press.

the screening assessment signaled that Max was not decoding at the expected level of a second grader—and that this risk was individual rather than a trait of his group—but it was the diagnostic assessment that provided more specific information on how that problem manifests in the real world. At the same time, the screening assessment allowed the teacher to be strategic in allocating time to do a running record with a student identified as "at risk" by the assessment battery.

Cataloguing Assessment Data to Support the At-Risk Reader

Once you've moved through the different stages of assessment, it's important to take the time to carefully consider the needs of the at-risk reader. Figure 4.3 catalogues some of Max's needs; Form 4.1 (at the end of the chapter) is a blank risk profile that can be used with any student. As you look through the example, you will see that it combines information from different assessments, with information that goes from the very broad to the increasingly specific. Information in this chapter is generally geared toward children who speak only English. If you have students who are simultaneously learning English and learning to read, you may want to read Chapter 5 before completing your own risk profile (Form 4.1).

Looking at Data to Monitor the Efficacy of Supplemental Instruction

Based on the analysis of assessment data, we are able to identify the goals for learning and the instructional content. Then once the supplemental instruction starts, we need to find out whether it's working! Every day, thousands of our readers like Max receive supplemental support that takes many different shapes and forms, addressing needs varying in nature from mild to severe. Whether it takes place as part of small-group instruction in the classroom, one on one for a few minutes before school each morning with the teacher, down the hall with the reading specialist, or even as part of a 3-week summer academy before the new academic year starts, we know that the collective efforts devoted to our strugglers are significant ones.

What we don't often know is just how well these supports are working and whether our time and efforts are well spent, so to speak. Despite significant resources devoted to supplemental supports and interventions, it's very rare that we actually find out if they're working. To do so, we need to use assessments

Student	Max
Instructional Profile	At risk in both code-based and meaning-related skills
Information from Test Booklets	Max moves through testing material quickly but makes a lot of errors. The errors he made on fluency passages disrupt the meaning of the passage; he also has difficulty with tracking and skipped lines of text more than once. His English vocabulary score was low.
Information from Diagnostic Assessment	In regular passages, Max reads most sight words correctly but misses nearly every multisyllabic word. He consistently mixes up word endings like -ing and -ed, and often loses his place in the passage. He reads with little expression, not stopping at periods or pausing at commas. His scores on vocabulary questions are in the middle range for the class. He seems to learn new words fairly well but does not usually apply them in his writing or speaking. He more often gets vocabulary questions right when there are multiple-choice items than open response. It is not clear if he understands books that are read aloud because he has not answered discussion questions.
Summary of Strengths and Difficulties	Max appears to have a solid sight-word vocabulary and is confident in common letter–sound combinations. However, he reads quickly and makes many errors while reading, particularly for longer words. He does not seem able to apply his knowledge of letter–sound relationships while reading new words and does not actively try to make meaning while reading.

FIGURE 4.3. Max's risk profile.

to track the progress of our strugglers beyond the usual assessments we might be using as part of our first tier of assessment. Once we've used assessment data to design an individualized plan for supports, there is a second function related to this second tier of assessment data—to monitor the impact of our efforts on the reader's skills. Importantly, it's not just about telling us whether our daily instructional effort or particular initiative *worked* or not; it's actually to find out, in real time, whether it's *working*. It tells us whether we need to make adjustments, or what we call midcourse corrections, to meet the needs of individual students who are struggling, and it regularly reminds us that time is of the essence to close gaps and meet all readers' needs. Toward this end (as noted in Chapter 3), we need to track strugglers' progress over time to:

- Determine whether students are *benefiting* appropriately from an instructional program.
- Identify students who are not demonstrating adequate progress.
- Build more effective instructional programs for students who are not benefiting.
- Compare the efficacy of different forms of instruction and design more effective, individualized instructional programs.

So, the teacher assesses the student's academic performance on a very regular basis (e.g., weekly, monthly), with the interval depending on the length of the intervention or the time frame for tailored instruction. Progress toward meeting the student's goals is measured by comparing how quickly the student is learning compared with what we might expect given the intensity of instruction. Based on these measurements, teaching is adjusted as needed. (For more on this design see Hosp et al., 2007; McKenna & Stahl, 2009.)

What about Our Struggling Readers Who Don't Respond to Classroom-Based Intervention?

By implementing data-driven literacy instruction that is guided by tiered assessment and instruction, we aim to improve academic performance and the classroom experience for students while simultaneously reducing the likelihood that some students are wrongly identified as having a disability. The tiered model of assessment and instruction is an imperative framework to ensure appropriate, timely identification of students with disabilities (Fuchs & Fuchs, 2005).

But in nearly any school or classroom, a small proportion of students do not respond to the combination of the core of instruction and supplemental supports—assessment data collected over time using multiple measures tells us that's the case. When students persistently show risk, or exhibit little or no growth over time despite significant and tailored additional instruction to meet their needs, these low scores become an indicator of the need for further investigation into their specific difficulties. These students may have learning or other disabilities. Therefore, following best practice, they receive an individualized, comprehensive evaluation to deeply investigate their profile (including strengths) as a learner and their ability levels in relation to what's expected given their age and grade level. At that time, written parental consent must be obtained. In interpreting the results, one guiding question focuses on their eligibility for special education services. We note that students should not be identified as having learning disabilities without an appropriate, comprehensive formal evaluation (Fuchs & Fuchs, 2005, 2006).

How does this process connect to classroom-based efforts to support this struggler? At this juncture, what has *already* happened with respect to classroom-based, additional supports and the corresponding data that has been collected over time becomes key information for this next step. The comprehensiveness and level of detail of information that has been collected by teachers and others who have supported the struggler will *greatly* impact the efficacy of the process and the likelihood of success in getting the persistent struggler to a better place as a reader.

Diagnostic and other data collected over the course of the interventions should be examined during the evaluation process, along with data from appropriately selected measures (e.g., tests of cognition, language, perception, and social skills). In this way, effective data-driven literacy instruction contributes to a comprehensive and detailed process of disability identification by reducing inappropriate identification of students who might appear to have a disability, but in fact have not received appropriate and/or adequate instruction.

Let's imagine, for example, that after several different instructional supports and approaches implemented in a number of different ways by well-trained adults, Max shows minimal response to these secondary or supplementary prevention efforts. Max should then be referred for formal evaluation. Eventually, in a meeting with the evaluation team, Ms. Perez shares the results of her careful documentation as well as her own professional insights focused on Max. In turn, the evaluation team (including the special education teacher and other qualified professionals) designs an evaluation that would identify a learning disability, should Max have one. In so doing, the team would rule out mental retardation as an alternative diagnosis (using a brief intellectual assessment) and eliminate other diagnostic possibilities for his persistent reading difficulties, such as a hearing impairment (though hopefully this has already been done along the way) or an emotional disturbance.

Bear in mind that while this process is underway Max will still be part of Ms. Perez's daily reading block. He may also continue in the same reading class even if he qualifies for special education services. That means we need to continue to focus on classroom-based supports designed to meet his needs. Should an individualized education plan (IEP) eventually be in place, Ms. Perez will likely be supported by others in the building. However, that she already knows Max as a reader and a child, combined with the information gleaned from the formal evaluation process, will greatly assist her efforts to move him to the next level, perhaps with more specialized supports. At this juncture, she will also revisit plans with Max's parents. Beyond the first level of targeted supports (often called Tier 2), services are generally considered to be special education, though students might receive this level of support without an IEP.

OTHER PIECES OF THE PIE: COULD IT BE SOMETHING MORE THAN JUST READING?

One year when Sky was teaching fourth grade she had a student whose reading difficulties seemed very mysterious. An intervention lesson showed growth but not at a rate that matched the level of effort and time that went into improving his reading. A special education evaluation found that the student had normal intelligence, with no processing or memory issues. Then one day his mother casually remarked that he had just broken another pair of glasses. A lightbulb went off. Glasses? She had never seen him wear glasses, not once. She did not even know he was supposed to have glasses. As it turned out, for the past several years he had taken off his glasses as soon as he was on the bus, then put them back on before he got home. The child was legally blind without his prescription (his uncorrected vision was around 20/200), and his desk was toward the back of the room.

While the effort it took to get the student to wear glasses in class every day is another story for a different book, making accommodations for his visual difficulties ultimately proved more effective than all of Sky's other efforts to promote his reading. Of course, there were no miraculous overnight transformations to top reader, and he still required intervention focused on his specific reading difficulties, but the pace of his progress picked up. Moreover, Sky felt she learned an important lesson: Sometimes the simplest issues can disrupt learning and these are easy to overlook. When working with struggling readers, it is to good check in physically and emotionally. Knowing whether a student is tired, hungry, upset over a conflict with peers, or facing major life transitions at home can help. We can work with parents to try to arrange an earlier bedtime, make sure the child gets breakfast before coming to class, or connect with a school counselor so that a child can join a group for students whose parents have recently divorced. However, it is important to be aware that addressing these issues does not typically resolve the reading difficulties. At-risk readers will still need a tiered instructional approach.

Conclusion

This chapter was written to help you begin to dig deeper into the data from your literacy assessment battery to support at-risk readers. For students who demonstrate individual risk, you will need to take several steps to further clarify the source of difficulties. The starting point is to identify the broad instructional profile of the student (i.e., difficulties with code-based and/or meaning-related skills), then to use all sources of data to hone in on specific issues for intervention. Once a plan for a struggling reader is in place and additional supports are underway, it's necessary to use assessments to monitor the effectiveness of the supports to determine whether a child is making gains as expected and ensure needed midcourse corrections are undertaken.

Taken together, these steps will allow you to identify instructional needs. Meeting those needs is the focus of Part III (Chapters 6, 7, and 8) of this book. If a child struggles persistently despite different supplemental approaches, as discussed, formal evaluation for additional services may be necessary. A decision tree is a useful tool for indicating whether a student needs additional assessment. Figure 4.4 is an example we created that could be modified depending on your school's approach.

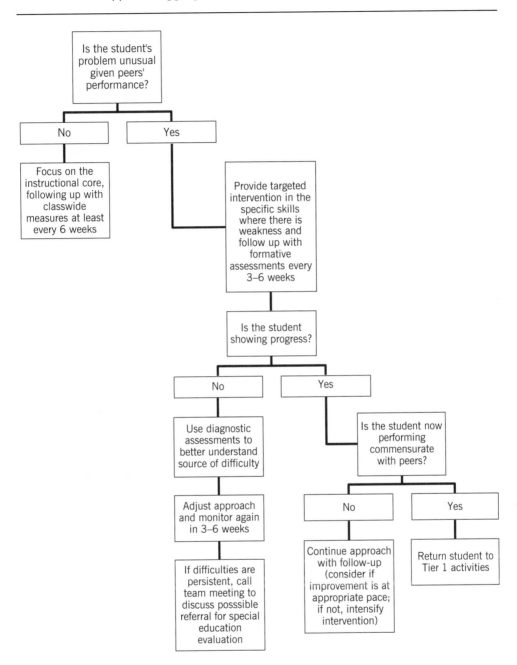

FIGURE 4.4. Decision tree for additional tiers of assessment.

FORM 4.1

Risk Profile (Resource Version)

Student	
Instructional Profile	
Information from Test Booklets	
Information from Diagnostic Assessment	
Summary of Strengths and Difficulties	

CHAPTER 5

Considerations for Linguistically Diverse Students

Linda Nguyen, a kindergarten teacher at Rosa Parks Elementary, remembers teaching Marcia like it was yesterday. When she sees her in the hallway today, she quickly flashes back to a shy but eager young girl with big brown eyes and a long ponytail. She was one of those students who only comes around every so often—eager to learn, quick to pick up her letter names, and the first to be on the carpet for a read-aloud. On top of that, she must have had the biggest smile in her class. It was clear to Linda that Marcia was well cared for at home and encouraged to work hard by her parents (both of whom moved to the United States from the Dominican Republic as young adults). It was usually her mother who dropped Marcia off and her grandfather who picked her up, often taking a few minutes to let her show him the day's work, with all conversation between them in Spanish. Marcia had come to Rosa Parks Elementary from the nearby public preschool, staffed by many who speak Spanish, where her mother had enrolled her when she started working outside the home. From these early years, it appears to Linda that Marcia has experienced a good deal of success in school. A storyteller by nature, her poems and stories have often been displayed in the school's hallways, and colleagues who taught her in subsequent years confirmed that she performed well on early reading indicators.

Now a 5th grader, Marcia's effort and radiant smile still ring true of Linda's impressions from years ago, but her grades are on a steady decline. Every morning she turns in neatly completed homework assignments, but Marcia increasingly misses answers and seems confused by schoolwork. During science and social studies she has begun to retreat behind her long, dark hair, almost as if to protect herself from having to participate in class discussions. She is increasingly quiet and timid in the classroom.

Marcia is a common story in classrooms in industrialized nations all over the world. She is part of a fast-growing group of children who come from homes where the primary language is not the societal language. In the United States, Canada, and Great Britain, for example, these learners are often referred to as ELLs, ESL speakers, and/or English as an additional language (EAL) speakers. In the United Kingdom, there are approximately 600,000 EAL students, who, together, represent 9% of the student population. In Canada, according to the 2006 Census, second-generation children make up 15% of the population. As of the 2000 Census in the United States, children of immigrants constituted 20% of the child population in the United States, and their numbers are growing seven times faster than those of latter-generation children (Schmidley, 2001; Shields & Behrman, 2004). Growth trends indicate that by 2050, 34% of children in the United States will be immigrants or children of immigrants (Passel & Cohn, 2008). Although the great majority of ELLs, like Marcia, have Spanish as their native language, together, the estimated 10.9 million ELL students in the United States speak over 400 different languages (National Center for Education Statistics, 2010). And Marcia is also part of a specific and the fastest growing cohort within the population of children of immigrants—she is U.S.-born and has come up through the education system without interruption.

Marcia's current homeroom teacher, Bob Thompson, is a well-respected veteran teacher. However, he is not entirely sure what to make of Marcia. On the one hand, Marcia is still performing better than many of her peers; on the other, she does not seem to be living up to her potential, and her steady—if not stark—decline is concerning. Bob is not sure what role her Spanish-speaking background plays in her school performance, and whether her confusion is a part of learning English that she will outgrow over time. At the same time, he wonders whether something is happening at home or with friends that is distracting her from the academic tasks at hand; he has certainly seen students' attention pulled away from the classroom at this age. What he can clearly tell is that Marcia wants to do well in school. He has often commented that if all of his students were as motivated as Marcia he would have an easy job, but now he worries whether that motivation is enough.

ELLs in Context

Linguistically diverse students are a vulnerable population within the PreK–12 system. In schools, teachers and principals are grappling with how to embed language instruction in the mainstream curriculum so as to best serve these students. Instructional leaders and superintendents are struggling with the demands of the accountability system to increase test scores among their population of ELLs. Schools often struggle to identify and implement the best practices for students who are faced with the challenge of learning to read in a language in which they are not fully proficient. Accordingly, these learners are struggling at high rates. For example, on a U.S. national assessment of reading comprehension in 2009, only 6% of 4th-grade language-minority learners receiving language support services scored at or above the proficient level compared with 34% of native English speakers (National Center for Education Statistics, 2010). In urban schools, many ELLs have fewer opportunities to learn than their peers, and in many cases their specific needs go unmet. A U.S. study conducted in California—the state with the highest number of ELLs in the country—showed that ELLs are subject to less developmentally appropriate practice than their native English-speaking peers, even within the same schools (Gándara & Rumberger, 2003). Other research has shown that the great majority of districts do not have services specially designed for ELLs with academic difficulties (Zehler et al., 2003). There is indication that these learners struggle in other countries as well. For example, 2009–2010 data from Ontario, Canada, where 21% of their student population speaks a language other than English and (like the United States) the majority are born in Canada, indicates that only 46% of third graders and 50% of sixth graders classified as ELL scored at or above the provincial standards in reading (Education Quality and Accountability Office, 2010). The data from the United Kingdom also suggests there is a performance gap between EAL students and native English speakers (UK Department of Education, 2010).

The statistic that shows ELLs to be the fastest-growing population of new enrollees in U.S. preschools and kindergartens is an especially important one in the context of planning for data-driven instruction to serve *all* students. Nonie's line of research has helped to shed light on the need to attend to these students not just through formal ELL designation but by designing more language-rich instruction to promote text comprehension in the mainstream classroom. By the upper elementary years, most of these students—like Marcia—do not have a formal designation to receive support services for language development. After all, they have been conversing in English in school since they were young children. Instead, they are learners who have been identified as having sufficient English proficiency for participation in mainstream classrooms without specialized support. However, many of these students have generally good foundational skills for word reading and many even read fluently, yet don't understand deeply what they read. These are students who have good conversational English skills but lack much of the academic language that is central to success with text and school, as we might suspect is the case for Marcia.

Some of Nonie's research sheds light on this problem. You might recall the diagram (Figure 2.2) in Chapter 2, containing Nonie's research findings from a study with U.S.-born children of immigrants who were enrolled in U.S. preschools at ages 3 and 4. We have found that as early adolescents their word-reading scores are well within the average range but their vocabulary levels are very low (Mancilla-Martinez & Lesaux, 2011). We also identified this same profile with another sample of early adolescents who entered U.S. schools in the primary grades (Lesaux & Kieffer, 2010). The same reader profile has been found in Canadian research with adolescents who entered school as young ELLs (Jean & Geva, 2009). Ultimately, low vocabulary levels are insufficient to support effective reading comprehension and writing, and in turn have a negative impact on overall academic success.

A challenge for school districts in many industrialized nations is to infuse more knowledge and expertise into their school systems in order to meet the needs of linguistically diverse learners. To address this pressing need, assessment-based, data-driven instruction is a very good starting place; however, in designing any assessment-driven literacy instructional framework, ELLs need special consideration.

An Assessment-Based Instructional Model for ELLs

Isn't a good assessment-based instructional model ideal for all students, including ELLs? The simple answer to this question is yes. But the rates at which this population is simultaneously growing in number and failing in our school system suggests we are most definitely not meeting their needs. Accordingly, we need to pay very careful attention to our assessment and instructional practices going forward. Given the overlap between the ELL and the struggling-reader populations, coupled with the role that language often plays in reading difficulties, it's important to spend some time highlighting three best practices for literacy assessment as they relate to this group of learners.

Multiple Measures for Multiple Purposes
(Especially When It Comes
to Oral Language Development)

As we've already outlined, not all available assessment tools and techniques are appropriate for all purposes. Any student assessment system must be comprehensive in nature, featuring multiple measures. Multiple assessments are very important in any RTI model, but especially when the model is used with linguistically diverse students. As we outlined in Chapter 1, it is how assessments are used and with whom and how the results are interpreted and used that can be positive or negative, accurate or inaccurate. The more data we generate, the more likely we are to better understand the reader.

The concept that different assessments serve different purposes, as discussed in Chapter 3, is even more important for ELLs, a group that routinely participates in separate language-proficiency assessments, either in addition to or in place of the general literacy assessment battery. Unfortunately, states and districts undoubtedly use these assessments for other purposes for which they are not designed. For instance, some districts routinely use an oral proficiency measure to inform decisions about interventions for struggling ELLs, even though their intended purpose is for initial placement, annual monitoring, and reclassification as it relates to English language development. Given the test properties and the complexity of what we call language proficiency, a single assessment cannot possibly serve these multiple purposes well. That is, a test designed strictly to identify whether a learner is above or below the redesignation threshold is not going to be sensitive enough to make the fine distinctions necessary for tailoring instruction to students' needs, such as identifying beginning and early intermediate students. In practice, it's not unusual for students like Marcia to be lumped into the same program as students who are just beginning to learn English. Moreover, this same test will provide little or no meaningful information on which to base interventions for individual children who are struggling, especially in the complex combination of code-based and meaning-related skills that are necessary for reading.

It's important to close this section with a specific piece of guidance. Even though in recent years we have seen improvements in the tests used to evaluate and monitor ELLs' English proficiency, and improvement in the way tests are used, ELLs will still need to participate in a comprehensive literacy assessment battery in addition to assessments designed to broadly gauge English listening and speaking skills.

Understanding and Addressing the Roots of Reading Difficulties

A robust body of research tells us that the great majority of ELLs (representing many different native languages) develop code-based skills that are equally as accurate and fluent as those of their classmates. In other words, they tend to develop foundational word-reading skills to age-appropriate levels without any significant delays (August & Shanahan, 2006). Although it may be counterintuitive, this means that we can hold ELLs to the same expectations for code-based skills as their peers who have only experienced English, and they can generally benefit from the same best practices in the instructional core. After all, much of the work that goes into decoding does not require understanding the word; thus, as skilled adult readers we can read words like *coabation* without connecting the print to a word we recognize. A very critical implication is that an ELL who struggles with code-based skills signals a need for instructional intervention that is separate from language learning. These problems usually will not resolve on their own as the child learns English but instead require intervention—in the same manner as their English-only classmates.

However, recent research tells us that this text-reading fluency may not be a reliable indicator of reading comprehension for ELLs. Specifically, studies in Canada and the United States with ELLs and their classmates, from primary grades through the sixth grade, show that students' text-reading fluency scores were in the average range yet their scores in reading comprehension were well below average (Jean & Geva, 2009; Lesaux, Crosson, Kieffer, & Pierce, 2010; Crosson & Lesaux, 2010; Lesaux & Kieffer, 2010). Generally speaking, many ELLs fit an instructional profile of needing intensive instruction in meaning-related skills, even when their code-based skills are proficient. Progress monitoring measures of fluency can only offer insight into fluency as a specific skill and should not be used as a proxy for overall reading achievement for any student. This is especially the case for ELLs.

It is important to realize that the same ELLs who score in the average range on measures of text-reading fluency often need significant support to develop English vocabulary knowledge and reading comprehension skills. This profile has implications for designing effective assessment to drive instruction. Of course, this profile cannot just be assumed but is a developmental trend that educators should bear in mind. As with any of our students, before assuming where a difficulty lies we first need to uncover their profile; for all students, but especially for ELLs, we need to supplement text-reading fluency measures with assessments in the domains of language and reading comprehension for effective screening and/or progress monitoring. Second, in classrooms with large numbers of ELLs we need to attend to this profile when designing our instructional core (discussed below and in Chapter 6). In such schools and classrooms, assessment of basic skills must be complemented by assessment in the domains of language, vocabulary, and reading comprehension to guide tailored and appropriate instruction in these areas.

Progress Monitoring Tells Us What Is Working for ELLs

As discussed in Chapters 3 and 4, once we have a comprehensive battery, progress monitoring is a key feature in any assessment system for assessing students' academic progress and for evaluating the effectiveness of instruction. As shown in Table 5.1, there are many questions to be asked and answered when designing a progress monitoring system for use in classrooms with ELLs, and also when looking at progress monitoring data designed to tell us how our ELLs are doing.

Narrowing In: The At-Risk ELL and the Multidimensional Nature of Oral Language

As discussed in Chapter 3, different assessments—even in the same domain—capture somewhat different skills and knowledge. Like reading comprehension, oral language is a multifaceted construct and many skills go into what we might call a student's "oral proficiency." We need to avoid thinking about ELLs' profiles in broad terms, such as "low" language skills, and instead generate an understanding of their relative skills—their strengths and their weaknesses—in specific domains of language in order to inform instruction and intervention efforts. This is especially important to know because second-language acquisition is an uneven developmental process. Some skills might develop more quickly than others; for example, some ELLs with good vocabulary knowledge might still have difficulty with grammar (or vice versa).

Therefore, for an assessment system to guide instructional improvement for ELLs, the process is twofold. First, as previously discussed (above and in Chapter 2), it must include meaning-related measures of language and comprehension. Second, we remind the reader that in designing an assessment battery to identify a student's developmental profile, we must recognize the many facets of broad skill areas. Rather than rely upon one measure of oral language proficiency, the assessment battery should attend to different facets of oral language. Whether you use standardized and published assessments, curriculum-based measures, or locally developed assessments, we recommend selecting and interpreting assessments in consultation with the ELL/ESL

TABLE 5.1. Important Questions about Progress Monitoring and ELLs

1. *Do our student assessment data show that most ELLs are making progress in general education?*
   - When most ELL students are struggling in reading, this is a systemic issue; it is likely that general education instruction does not match needs and/or lacks sufficient intensity.
   - Teachers and school leaders can use data to determine when it is necessary to adjust instruction for ELLs.

2. *Is the progress monitoring element of our RTI model one component of a comprehensive evaluation for ELLs who are struggling?*
   - Teachers and school leaders should use data to determine when it is necessary to adjust instruction for ELLs who are struggling.

3. *Do we have a working sense of which measures are more sensitive and less sensitive to ELLs' growth?*
   - Because there are very few studies of progress monitoring with linguistically diverse students, it is important for districts and schools to undertake their own comparisons and analyses to determine how their ELLs are faring and what the typical patterns of growth and development are (see Chapter 3 for further discussion of longitudinal data).

4. *Do we have a working sense of how ELLs' performance is influenced on particular measures by individual and classroom characteristics? Do we examine their error patterns?*
   - The similarities between students' native language and English will influence their language and reading abilities, particularly in the areas of phonological awareness and phonics (e.g., ELLs may have trouble discriminating between auditory sounds not present in their language; students who learn to read in Spanish may segment at the syllable level rather than the phoneme level).

5. *Where possible and appropriate, for those receiving native-language instruction, are we using native-language measures to assess our ELLs' skills and shed light on sources of difficulties?*
   - While native-language assessment can shed light on sources of difficulties, it is only under specific circumstances that this proves useful. These circumstances include but are not limited to formal opportunities to develop the native language in an academic setting, and a highly trained bilingual individual to administer and interpret the scores.

6. *Have we considered dynamic approaches to assessment within the RTI framework?*
   - Assessments that involve preassessment, teaching, and postassessment can provide important insights into students' needs and their learning potential.

Note. Based on Sáenz (2008) and Klingner, Soltero-Gonzalez, and Lesaux (2010).

department or another district department with expertise in ELL assessment. We also recommend gaining detailed insight into the information provided by the standards-based language-proficiency measures.

These domains include but are not limited to vocabulary, grammar/syntax, morphological skills (i.e., understanding of word forms and parts), language-processing skills (e.g., phonological awareness), and oral comprehension. In the domain of vocabulary, linguistically diverse students often have receptive vocabularies that are much larger than their expressive (or productive) vocabularies. That is, they can understand what they hear more readily than they can express their ideas through speaking or writing. This also is the case with many native speakers. Additionally, ELLs might have a broad but not very deep vocabulary, such as only having one meaning for words that have multiple meanings. For example, ELL students may be confused when a character "brushes off" disappointment, because they may only connect *brush* to the common meaning of *hairbrush*. ELLs also tend to be confused by referents (e.g., pronouns), prepositions (e.g., *on, behind*), and cohesion markers (e.g., *however, therefore*; August & Shanahan, 2006; Crosson, Lesaux, & Martiniello, 2008). Here, we suggest administering written or oral prompts to generate writing samples and to assess oral narrative skills and in turn, gain insight into children's grammatical skills, word knowledge, and overall language development.

Many districts and schools have particular prompts to administer to all students; looking closely at students' work and comparing work across students can provide important insights about development. Just as teachers differentiate their instruction, assessment must focus on capturing subtle shifts in English proficiency levels and assessments that focus on providing diagnostic information. For example, when a student like Marcia begins to use the words she has learned in class in her writing, she is displaying growth that may not be captured on a formal assessment of vocabulary. Samples of student work provide a rich starting point for discussing instruction. Is Marcia using words that have been explicitly taught in class? What weaknesses in grammar emerge through her writing? In responding to text, what aspects of its meaning does she seem to grasp?

Conclusion

Learning to read and write while also gaining proficiency in a language presents a big challenge for students. The ideal assessment battery will help target language supports while also providing a clear understanding of development of both code-based and meaning-related reading skills. These formal assessments are best supplemented with diagnostic assessments that invite analysis of performance in authentic context, as well as progress monitoring assessments that follow the student over time (for further discussion see Chapter 6). With such a system in place, we can best support our growing population of students who arrive at school with the everyday adjustment challenges that come with school entry, but with the additional challenge of having to learn in a language that they are not proficient in. For those ELLs who appear to be struggling with reading development in a significant and persistent manner, their issues may run beyond those of second-language learning. To that end, we refer back to Chapter 4 where we address relevant issues that should be considered with those presented here.

PART III

Action Steps
for Improved Instruction

CHAPTER 6

Identifying Instructional Priorities and Designing Effective Instruction

It was such a mild, balmy late-fall day that Sharona Jackson enjoyed playground duty as an opportunity to be outside. She was always interested in the way that her first-grade students behaved outside the classroom; today she found herself watching Kim. The little girl stood alone near the fence, pulling the seeded heads off of dandelions that had wedged their way up through the concrete, plucking out each individual white seed in turn, lost in her own world. Nearby, a group of her classmates, all girls, were blowing the dandelion fluff at each other in a made-up game that apparently involved running away to avoid being touched by the seeds. Kim was so near yet so far from the happy camaraderie of the group. Today was not the only day she played by herself—Kim was one of only a few of Sharona's students who did not appear to have any friends.

Sharona sighed, wondering what she could do to help Kim. Social issues notwithstanding, Kim was academically advanced and a top student. She entered kindergarten already reading, apparently having taught herself at home. As a first grader, she read chapter books that were more often assigned to second or third graders, like *Captain Underpants* (Pilkey, 1997) and the *Amber Brown* series by Paula Danziger. Sharona had recently initiated the referral process for Kim to be evaluated for the gifted program.

Being advanced, however, did not make school fun and rewarding for Kim—nor was she an easy student. Kim had a way of flopping down on the rug for story time with the same dramatic unhappiness another child might display going to the dentist. At the beginning of the year she had dominated story discussions, calling out answers instead of raising her hand, emphasizing how "easy" the questions were. A wrong answer from a classmate would often elicit a roll of the eyes and quick correction from Kim, whose reputation for being bossy followed her from kindergarten. After Sharona had worked with Kim on appropriate behavior during rug time, the interruptions and responses ended. Now Kim was simply checked out. She could always answer a question if called upon or pressed, often with amazing sophistication; otherwise, she contented herself to drawing pictures on the rug with her finger, fiddling with her clothes, or simply staring off into space. She was happiest during independent work, when left alone with a book from one of her beloved series.

When the new assessment battery was initiated at Rosa Parks Elementary, Sharona was glad for the chance to learn more about her students as readers. However, when she heard that the school would start to use the data to differentiate instruction beginning at the core—the lessons that all students received during the literacy block—she immediately thought about Kim. What would this new plan *really* do for her? While there were certainly a good number of first graders in her class with clear and pressing instructional needs, Sharona firmly believed that Kim had needs too. And it worried her to think that Kim was becoming disenchanted with school because it moved at the pace of the slowest student. Every year Sharona wrestled with the challenge of making sure all of her students received instruction in the concepts and skills that would be important for them to succeed in second grade, and the last thing she wanted was to reduce her expectations for any student. Sharona was definitely unsure about how she might use data to change her core instruction, and thereby meet the needs of *every* student.

Using assessment results to differentiate instruction is no easy task. We know that children as young as 4 and 5 enter school already displaying big differences in language comprehension and early literacy skills (Dickinson & Tabors, 2001; Hart & Risley, 1995). So how can we provide appropriate instruction to a whole group of students when their abilities cover such a wide range? And how can we keep pace with learning standards and curriculum when students are not mastering material? These are some of the most complex issues facing Sharona and her counterparts across the globe.

In this chapter, we watch as Sharona moves through a process of differentiating her literacy block for her particular group of students. It begins with Sharona using the results of the schoolwide screening and progress monitoring assessment battery to identify a priority area of instructional need for the entire group. Her next step is attempting to understand best practices in the identified (priority) domain. Third, she takes stock of her current practice in that domain, both in terms of time allocation and the materials she used. Her final step is to identify learning opportunities across the literacy block, for all students, including small-group work. Screening assessments are used to better diagnose student needs and to provide input on the effectiveness of her strategy. Through this four-step process (shown in Figure 6.1), the data becomes a source of support for Sharona's teaching, helping her meet the needs of all her students, including Kim.

Step 1: Identifying the Primary Needs of the Group

As a first step in analyzing student data, it is often more powerful to identify the overall needs of our classrooms than to focus on individual students. Individual needs are important, to be sure. However, a tiered instructional model works best and serves the greatest number of students when there is a strong core of instruction—one that has already been adapted from the general guidance provided in curriculum and standards to fit the group of learners congregated within a particular classroom setting. After all, our students do not receive instruction in isolation but are part of a community of students filling our classrooms and schools, often from the same neighborhoods. At the level of the student population, this shared background shapes students' needs, resulting in some collective strengths and weaknesses. Although it is paramount to meeting students' needs, differentiating the core of instruction (i.e., the lessons all students receive in the literacy block) is often an overlooked step in instructional planning. It is, however, what allows us to begin to mold our teaching routines and curriculum to support and challenge our learners.

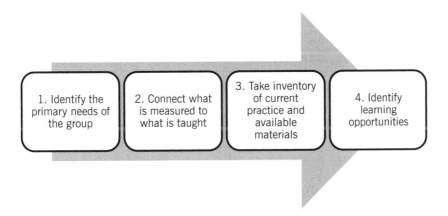

FIGURE 6.1. Four-step process to differentiate the literacy block.

For Sharona, this means taking a step back from Kim and thinking about her entire first-grade classroom—for the time being. We will return to Kim at Step 4 in the process. In the meantime, the results of her class of 22 students on the screening measures of the fall assessment battery are listed in Table 6.1. In every domain there are students whose results suggest they are on track (or perhaps even working far above expectations, like Kim) and others who are performing poorly. When looking at student test scores the first impulse many of us have is to look at individual students. We want to see how each student performed and try to gain a fine-grained understanding of specific difficulties.

But what about the group? To be more effective and efficient, when we first look at literacy data we must gain a big-picture understanding of both our students' aptitudes and our own instructional strengths and weaknesses. Again, our very first level of differentiation should be for the classroom (or even school, depending upon your role) in order to provide the best possible core of instruction (Tier 1). Take a second look at Table 6.1, focusing on the

TABLE 6.1. Looking at Student Risk

Name	Code based		Meaning related	
	Letter identification	Phonics	Receptive vocabulary	Listening comprehension
Ana	Some risk	High risk	High risk	High risk
Bailey	Low risk	High risk	High risk	High risk
Chris	High risk	High risk	High risk	High risk
Curtis	Low risk	High risk	High risk	High risk
Devonte	Low risk	Low risk	Some risk	Low risk
Elian	Low risk	Low risk	High risk	Some risk
Georgia	Some risk	Low risk	High risk	Some risk
Harold	Low risk	Some risk	Low risk	High risk
Isaac	Low risk	Low risk	High risk	Low risk
Josiah	Low risk	Low risk	Low risk	Low risk
Kim	Low risk	Low risk	Low risk	Low risk
Kimberlee	Some risk	High risk	Low risk	Some risk
Leander	Low risk	Low risk	Low risk	Low risk
Monique	Low risk	Low risk	Some risk	High risk
N'Shawn	Low risk	Low risk	Some risk	High risk
Oliver	Low risk	Low risk	Some risk	High risk
Patrick	Low risk	Low risk	Some risk	High risk
Renee	Low risk	Low risk	Some risk	High risk

columns—these are the skill areas measured by each test—rather than on the rows, or students. Within each column we can begin to see how many students are struggling in a particular skill area. Our view shifts from the individual patterns to the collective trends. The chart in Figure 6.2 summarizes the level of risk displayed by students in the domains the assessment battery measured. Charts such as these are very useful in quickly identifying areas of greatest need for the overall group, and help us, in this first step, to focus on trends over individuals.

What do you notice? Sharona saw that nearly all of her students knew their letters in line with expectations for the beginning of first grade. This finding helped confirm something she already knew about her students; specifically, that many had attended kindergarten and had mastered some of the more foundational aspects of reading. What emerged as a problem area for many of them, however, was listening comprehension—*half* of the students were at very high risk in listening comprehension and over 60% displayed a level of risk! Vocabulary was the second-greatest area of need. In general, we find that students tend to have greater needs in meaning-related skills than code-based skills.

Form 6.1 (at the end of the chapter) is designed to assist in identifying the location of greatest instructional need in a classroom. Sharona has identified meaning-related skills as a priority area for instruction, particularly since many of her students struggled on both of the meaning-making measures (listening comprehension and vocabulary). However, focusing on meaning making does

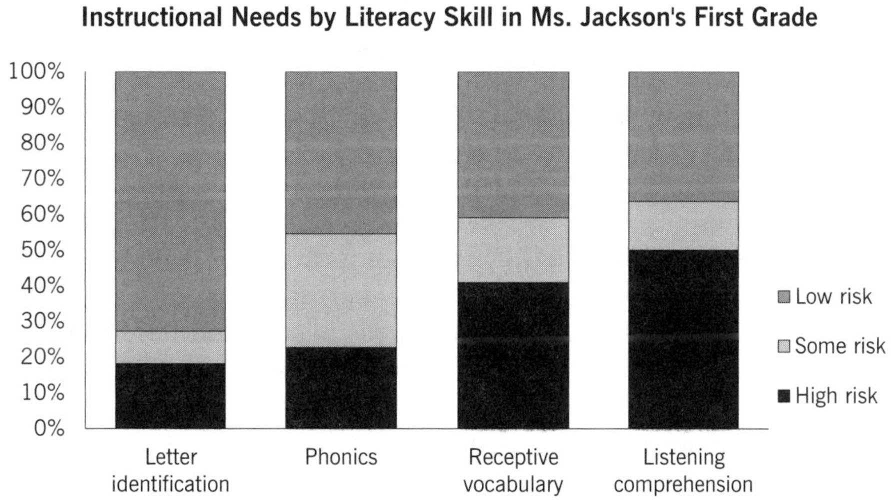

Instructional Needs by Literacy Skill in Ms. Jackson's First Grade

FIGURE 6.2. Looking at classroom risk.

not mean she will abandon other areas of instruction; rather, she will actively examine the skills that go into listening comprehension and how she teaches those skills. Again, the goal here is to create the best possible instruction for promoting these meaning-related skills within her instructional day and utilizing the materials at hand. During the next assessment period for the whole class, she can determine whether to continue with this focus, or whether it is time to move on to another aspect of literacy instruction. Answer the questions shown in Form 6.1 to start to understand and identify student performance within the context of the school and classroom.

The broad priority area identified through an assessment battery provides a jumping-off point for further exploring practice and student needs. Sharona now has a priority focus on meaning-related skills and can use it to better understand student needs in her classroom. Still, while the data make clear that her students require instruction that will boost their listening comprehension skills, it is not immediately clear what exactly her instructional response should be. She thought back to the new assessment battery and the listening comprehension measure in particular. When the students "took" the measure, they listened to a story and then answered questions. So, her initial knee-jerk response was to have students listen to stories more often and answer questions. But then she thought about Kim, who was already bored with listening to stories and answering questions. And what about the student who sits quietly through the story but does not participate in discussion afterward?

Sharona's concerns and questions are good ones. Next, we discuss the important and surmountable challenge that Sharona faces in turning these scores into effective changes in her daily practice.

Step 2: Connecting What Is Measured to What Is Taught

We know that Sharona's initial response—to teach in the same manner and format as the test—is a predictable response, especially when data are not coupled with sufficient training. This brings us to one of the trickiest aspects of using data to inform our instructional approach: Data-driven instruction is not inherently good or useful. Much needs to be in place for it to support teacher and student progress; indeed, there is clear documentation of data-driven instruction gone awry (e.g., Goodman, 2006, presents a collection of examples around misuses of the DIBELS). As shown in Figure 6.3, very often the data-driven instruction gone-bad scenarios involve a context where heavy emphasis is placed on a single assessment and practitioners go into overdrive

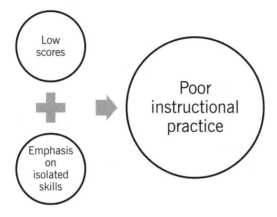

FIGURE 6.3. The case for balanced assessment.

to increase performance on an isolated skill that is measured by the assessment. Instruction shifts from our bigger goals for our students as readers to focusing exclusively on a single indicator of progress. In the meantime, other important areas of literacy do not receive their due. When instruction becomes overly focused on isolated skills, children who are at risk of reading difficulties in other areas fall further behind, and children who might otherwise reach benchmarks may even develop risk. This does not happen because the assessment is problematic but because it is not implemented or interpreted appropriately.

Adapting instruction from assessment results is where the art of teaching meets the science of teaching. For screening assessments, such as those shown here, the testing situation for the student is and should be very different from the teaching situation (see Chapter 3)—they are driven by very different goals. We know that robust, cohesive instruction requires more than simply listening to stories and answering questions. After all, screening assessments are (by design) narrow. They use specific behaviors to gauge performance in areas that require coordination of a broad array of skills—skills that go far beyond those used in the test. Therefore, instruction needs to cast a far wider net than any given assessment and take into account the areas involved in skill development that are not necessarily obvious to the test onlooker. That is, the instructional needs revealed by low scores are far broader than what is suggested by the procedures involved in the testing situation, or even the score reports. To provide excellent instruction, Sharona must really understand what skills underlie listening comprehension. Further, she must identify learning experiences that actively and authentically engage students in developing those skills.

A Pedagogical Challenge

Making this leap from scores to effective lessons is probably the biggest challenge the teacher faces. In Sharona's case, rather than thinking of listening comprehension as an isolated "skill," we know that she needs to understand that listening comprehension serves as a proxy for some important meaning-related skills, including vocabulary, background knowledge, and even familiarity with stories and texts. In this case, meaning-related skills then become the instructional priority. A similar path would be necessary if her students had struggled in sounding out non-words—these would serve as a proxy for needing intensified instruction in code-based skills that would extend far beyond sounding out non-words.

Contrast two examples in Sky's teaching experience that demonstrate the importance of understanding assessment results and how to connect them appropriately to practice. One year, when she was teaching fourth grade, her district implemented a new assessment in which students read a cloze passage on a computer screen and selected the best word or sentence to fill in the blank from a list of options. The test produced a class list with each student's estimated grade level in reading. In the first year, Sky found the results confusing and her students' parents often found them upsetting—understandably, nobody wanted to find out their fourth grader was reading at a 1.3 grade level. That said, in their book on literacy assessment to understand the individual, Michael McKenna and Katherine Stahl (2009) make a good argument that grade equivalents are the least useful score. Because it was not very clear to Sky what the test measured, or what it meant for practice, what made sense to her at the time was to focus in on the cloze procedure the test employed. This was not for lack of caring for her students, nor was it driven by a desire to "teach to the test." Rather, she felt it must be important for students to understand how to fill in cloze passages if it was tested and the results were discussed at length. Her understandable but undesirable response was to spend a great deal of time crafting cloze passages for her students to practice. Indeed, she even sought to "differentiate" her instruction by creating cloze passages at different reading levels.

In a subsequent year, following on more work and training on the assessment, Sky again had many fourth-grade students with low scores on the same measure. This time, she understood that the important element of the assessment was not its format (i.e., a cloze passage) but that it was an indicator of reading comprehension. As the assessment results came in, her students were about to read *My Side of the Mountain* (George, 1959), a book about a young boy who leaves home to live in a hollowed-out hemlock tree. The book was assigned as part of the reading program and it was a daunting prospect for Sky to teach her students, who lived in the desert in New Mexico, to connect with the story of a boy living in a large tree in the middle of a deep forest. However, she worked to incorporate the best practices she was learning about reading comprehension: building background knowledge on the topic, explicit instruction in key vocabulary, using graphic organizers to discuss story structure and ideas, and exploring important ideas in the story through discussion and writing. The assigned book became a cornerstone in a thematic, cross-curricular unit on wilderness survival. The unit was structured around a central question of what it takes to survive in different settings, including a direct link to science standards requiring that students learn about different ecosystems.

At the end of the year, guess which classroom of fourth graders performed better on the state standardized test? The ones who discussed how the main character from their novel would have had to adapt to survive on the tundra, or those who dutifully filled in blanks of texts that were at their measured reading level but not connected to larger ideas? Even more importantly, guess which group had better attendance, spent more time on task in class, and were just generally more excited to read? The second scenario clearly presents better instruction and did, in fact, result in higher scores on outcome measures. However, it was several steps removed from the assessment, and not focused on individual student needs. Instead, it represents an enriched approach to whole-group instruction. Instead of disenfranchising students, like Kim, who were advanced, this approach made top students more involved. And while there were certainly students who needed support to access the level of text difficulty in the assigned book, students with greater instructional needs were also supported. They were supported through the exploration of the topic and words that provided greater background knowledge on the book. Tweaking the core of instruction made the classroom more inclusive—far different from Sharona's concern that "differentiation" results in lower expectations.

Professional Learning

So how do we make these connections between assessment and instruction? Creating an instructional approach requires reflection, professional development, and ideally discussion within a professional learning community. Sharona already had some good ideas around comprehension strategies. For example, she knew that good comprehension instruction—that will be captured in a listening comprehension measure—involves guiding students in making text-to-self connections and in actively monitoring their own thinking as they approach the story (i.e., metacognition). Direct instruction in comprehension strategies, such as making predictions and visualizing what is happening in the story, also helps build listening comprehension. At the same time, Sharona wanted to know more about the skills underlying comprehension, especially the listening comprehension format.

The approach an individual teacher (or school) takes toward professional learning will be personal and depend on the resources at hand. Sometimes resources are available within the school building, including a reading specialist or coach, an experienced or exceptional teacher who can model lessons or allow observations, a professional learning community within the school, a principal who can serve as an instructional leader, or even a grade-level team that is committed to widening its perspective. In other cases, the district may be able to offer coaches or workshops, or there may be a highly effective school or classroom nearby to visit. At other times, it may be best for educators to attend conferences or workshops away from the school, or to find some key resources like books or Internet sites as a basis for discussion—perhaps even classes at a local university. The important element is not where or how the professional learning takes place but that it is targeted to the key areas of instructional need identified through the assessment process; it is crucial that educators approach professional learning with a clear goal for their own work.

Step 3: Taking Inventory of Current Practice and Available Materials

With a priority area for instruction identified through the screening element of the literacy battery and fueled by her own observations and diagnostic assessments, Sharona is ready to begin making changes to her instructional routines. One of the first steps in working with Sharona was to take inventory of her current literacy block and how time is allocated within the day. Sharona described a typical day in the first grade:

- As students arrive at school, each signs in, puts away his or her belongings, and is then allowed to choose a center or eat breakfast from the cafeteria until the day officially begins with the morning announcements and the Pledge of Allegiance.
- Students then gather at the rug for morning meeting and the daily read-aloud.
- After the read-aloud, Sharona reviews the alphabet with students and then presents a mini-lesson on phonics and word work.

- Students then use a work board to find an assigned task, while Sharona works with small, guided groups.
- In the afternoon, students participate in Writer's Workshop.

In describing her daily instructional goals, Sharona discusses the need for students to become familiar with words by understanding the connection between letters and sounds, and how letter–sounds become words. She highlights the importance of children understanding stories and getting opportunities to read books that are at an appropriate level. Sharona fills out a chart (see Form 6.2 at the end of the chapter) that shows her primary teaching strategies in code-based and meaning-related skills.

The simple act of charting instructional time can help you identify how your literacy block fits with student needs. While it is important to continue to provide balanced instruction, you may find that more time could be "budgeted" toward certain key skill areas. You may also find adjustments that are needed in your teaching materials. For Sharona, she recognized that her students are likely to benefit from more time devoted to story discussion, even if that means 5 minutes are taken away from her work-board time. In fact, she realized that she may not need to review the alphabet with her entire class every day but continue that activity with the small group of students identified through the battery as needing help with letters.

In order to gain a really strong understanding of how instructional time is being invested, invite a colleague, mentor, or instructional leader to observe your teaching. Ask him or her to chart the time you spend on instruction: How many minutes are devoted to phonics, discussion questions, word work, and so on? You can compare the results to what you have charted to see whether the two match up, or what areas may be taking more time than expected. Discuss what students are doing during the literacy block with the goal of understanding how they spend the bulk of their instructional time. How do these activities relate to the identified area of need? What small adjustments hold the potential for big differences?

Step 4: Identifying Learning Opportunities

With new information at hand—or even after reflecting on what crucial practices routinely get crowded out in the course of a busy school day—the cyclical nature of examining practice in a data-driven system begins. Where are the opportunities in the day to intensify instruction? What is the strategy for making sure that the reading block is adapted for the students at hand?

In a typical elementary classroom, there are several key opportunities to intensify instruction in the literacy block. Again, the important factor here is the process. For each classroom in each school the needs of students will vary. In order to better understand what the process entails, however, we will follow Sharona as she creates an instructional strategy to support her first graders, based on the assessment data and her analysis of how she is using instructional time.

Digging Deeper: Making the Core Work for the Collective

Sharona began right away to look for clues as to why her students might have a hard time understanding what they read or what is read to them. She audiorecorded some of the story discussions to analyze students' responses and carefully looked over their written responses to story themes. These informal, diagnostic assessments gave her some critical information. For fiction stories on familiar topics, many of her students were able to answer general questions and follow the story structure (i.e., beginning, middle, and end) quite well. However, when the books centered on more obscure topics, or had an unusual setting or theme, many seemed confused, even if they enjoyed the book.

As suggested by the assessment data, underdeveloped background knowledge and vocabulary were, indeed, compromising many students' comprehension—why was that? While looking over the teacher's edition to her curriculum, she realized that the stories and books for guided reading were already grouped into loose thematic units but that she had never really capitalized on this structure. Working with her fellow first-grade teacher next door, Sharona began to put an emphasis on the overarching theme and tie in more books on related topics. This began with a unit focused on friendships, with some changes in the way that time was allocated within the literacy block. Using the overarching thematic connection, she brought in a few extra materials for read-alouds, always discussing how it connected to friends, as she had budgeted more time for discussion of read-alouds. However, she also reinforced the theme throughout the day. When students misbehaved, for example, she talked to them about ways they could be good friends to their classmates.

She began to widen the scope for the type of texts she brought in—poems, songs, greeting cards, even a newspaper article on old friends and some nonfiction books about friendship in the animal community. She directly tied the idea of friendships into social studies by talking about how groups could promote peaceful change. A piece of chart paper was used to web out different words for friends they encountered (e.g., *pal, buddy, confidante, comrade*), and students were asked to write sentences about friends using some of these new and different words during Writer's Workshop. They then created a class book on how to solve problems with friends, using some of the new vocabulary words and ideas they had absorbed through the unit, incorporating both reading and social studies.

While the overall structure of the reading block did not change, Sharona's new strategy meant that her read-alouds were more purposeful and incorporated more best practices. With the support of the thematic unit, her students were able to engage with more challenging material and entirely different types of texts. And even though this created a more supportive environment for some of her struggling readers, it also created a more challenging environment for Kim, who did not read nonfiction much at all and who certainly benefited from a unit on friendship—discussion around topics like how to cheer up a friend were new to her. The unit was particularly satisfying for Sharona because it included many socioemotional themes, and provided some new language for Kim, among others, to approach their classmates within casual conversation. After several weeks, she noticed that most of her students were able to respond better to questions anchored in text and there were some marked improvements in student writing—key indicators (and good diagnostic assessments) that her revised approach was a success.

Student Groupings

The new focus on making meaning of stories did not mean that the hard work of helping students read words was over, or that Sharona stopped meeting with groups. Some students needed extra practice with decoding skills, and these could not always be related back to the focus on meaning making. However, Sharona did put the results from the assessment battery to work in planning her small-group work. First, the results helped her create groups by identifying students' approximate levels. Second, she made sure that some of the small-group work did relate back to comprehension. For students who decoded too slowly to make meaning of texts, she began assigning them to listening centers and sometimes read them text to discuss. Thus, she was able to maintain an overall focus on making meaning of connected texts, even if it was not the entire focus.

Sharona also made one big change to her daily calendar: she shifted the time for work board to the end of the literacy block so that she could begin to collaborate with some of the other teachers in the building for student groups. She was able to get Kim into a second-grade classroom twice weekly for a reading group—a switch that delighted both Kim and her parents. Meanwhile, she and her first-grade partner worked together to share a group of their lowest students so that the group would get some instruction every single day.

School-to-Home Connections

Ultimately, the time Sharona has with her students each day is limited. In order to maximize student learning, it is helpful to create a strategy for connecting school and home, to extend students' learning beyond the classroom. While Sharona certainly had some students who did not have a great deal of home support, homework was taken seriously in many students' homes; these families looked to her as a source of guidance for promoting their child's development. In the past, Sharona had asked all of her students to keep a daily reading log, requesting that they read aloud or hear books for 20 minutes a day. These at-home reading experiences were recorded on the log, signed by a parent or guardian, and then returned to school. She decided to stay with this practice.

However, Sharona felt that this homework could also reinforce the story discussions she had been working on in class. She decided to translate this work into the home context by requesting that parents spend as much time discussing a story as they do reading stories. In her weekly newsletter, she is adding a new feature she calls "Ask Me about. . . . " This new feature includes a question related to classroom events and activities of the week. She hoped that this prompt would open a discussion for families, making homework more interactive.

Putting It Together

What are the action steps that teachers can take to implement the best instruction? We suggest an overarching approach that involves identifying student needs through data, finding the best practices in high-needs domains, finding opportunities to strengthen current practice, and then reflecting on practice. This approach does not suggest specific activities or programs but relies instead on reflective practice and professional development. After all, the field of literacy is always progressing; by the time you are reading this book, there may be new information about best practices, especially for certain student populations.

What we are proposing is a four-step process to connect data to practice. First, aggregate scores—the combined scores of a group of students—guide us in identifying key areas where students would benefit from an instructional boost by creating a classroom (or school) profile. The job of screening assessments is to identify these areas, not to address them. Once the assessments have done their job and we have analyzed and interpreted the scores, we must step away from the assessments and embark on the second step of identifying evidence-based practices. We then examine our instructional routines with an eye to how time and attention is allocated as our third step. The fourth and final task (see Form 6.3 at the end of the chapter) is to look for ideas and strategies to intensify instruction in the identified priority area throughout the literacy blocks and perhaps even the school day. All of these steps—administering a good battery, understanding scores, then connecting the identified needs to practice—are essential to maximizing student learning.

Classroom Performance Analysis: Self-Study

Student Performance in Context	
In my classroom, do more students struggle with code-based or meaning-related skills, or do a large percentage struggle with both?	
What are the specific skills for which the largest proportion of students display risk?	
What are the specific skills for which the fewest students display risk?	
Who are the students who display risk in areas when most of their peers meet benchmarks?	
Who are the students who score far higher than their peers? In what skills?	

Analyzing Current Classroom Practice

Literacy Component	Current Time Spent Teaching	Materials	Teaching Methods and Instructional Routines	Needed Changes to Support Instructional Priority
Phonological awareness (for preschool through first grade)	Daily			
	Weekly			
Phonics and fluency	Daily			
	Weekly			
Comprehension strategies	Daily			
	Weekly			
Vocabulary	Daily			
	Weekly			

FORM 6.3

Maximizing Meaningful Learning Opportunities across the Day

Priority Area

Setting	Current Practices	Ideas for Intensifying
Whole Class		
Small Groups		
Centers		
School to Home		

CHAPTER 7

Putting Schoolwide Response to Intervention in Place

Margarita Richards, Rosa Parks Elementary's newly hired literacy coordinator, sat in a school hallway, crouched down in a chair that came no higher than her knee. The table in front of her was neatly set up with testing materials and her clipboard. Also at the table was Shelly, a student from the school's 4-year-old PreK program, who fit far better in the chairs borrowed from the preschool classroom. The two sat corner to corner; Shelly was eager and excited. Each time Margarita said a word out loud, little Shelly would crinkle her face, sometimes tapping her head to show she was thinking. She would then point to a picture she thought best represented the word, looking up at Margarita with a smile as she made her choice. As they finished up, Margarita thanked Shelly for her hard work and gave her a sticker. Delighted, Shelly skipped ahead of Margarita back into the classroom, braids bouncing, sticker proudly displayed on her forehead.

Margarita followed Shelly into the classroom of preschool teacher Daisy Eckman. The system they had worked out to minimize distractions from testing wasn't quite working; every time Margarita came into the room, all eyes were on her. "Is it my turn? Is it my turn?" the children would ask, eager for their chance to spend one-on-one time with a special adult. A few came right up to her, pulling on her cardigan, one slipping his hand onto hers. "I'm looking for someone who is following directions," Margarita announced, forcing herself to put on a serious face as their little bodies made a big show of doing their activities. "Miss Daisy, Miss Daisy," said a young boy with elfin ears and big eyes. "Is it true that you have the same name as, as Ma'rita?" With that the room erupted into chatter about this exciting visitor, whose name was the Spanish version of their beloved teacher's name, and who spent time with each of them in turn, playing a word game and giving out stickers. Every time a child returned with his or her sticker and a report of the fun he or she had, it created more anticipation for those who just couldn't wait for a turn!

Margarita was head of a special team that was administering a vocabulary screening assessment to each student in the school, from the 4-year-olds to the fifth graders. The team was small, but their presence represented a big shift at Rosa Parks Elementary. Previously, individual teachers were charged with the responsibility of implementing data-driven instruction; now the school was working to create a cohesive, systematic schoolwide model of RTI for literacy. The goal was to ensure that all students were tested in a timely manner with sufficient turnaround to allow for interpretation of results and application to instruction. In theory, this would prevent any child at the school from "slipping through the cracks" with undetected problems, catalyzing early intervention before students developed real difficulties. The larger goal was improved instructional practices for all students—teaching that was targeted to students' needs.

In this chapter we focus on this critical next step of connecting scores generated from the comprehensive literacy battery to instructional practice across a school system. In essence, this involves taking the assessment-to-instruction cycle outlined in Chapter 6 to scale at a school or district level. In many ways this represents a culmination of all of the preceding chapters. In order to enact a strong RTI model, we have to ensure that we are measuring and monitoring the skills that impact reading achievement (see Chapter 2) with the appropriate tools (see Chapter 3). We need to make sure that we are using patterns in the data to differentiate core instruction (see Chapter 6) while providing targeted instruction to struggling readers (see Chapter 4). However, in this chapter we address the additional tasks of implementing schoolwide systems and structures to make an RTI model "click" across the various ages and professional needs of any elementary school.

The real-world struggles of Rosa Parks Elementary will again serve as a prototype for this complex process. Indeed, we use this chance to revisit our profile students—namely Carter, Marcia, Max, and Kim—to understand how their individual needs fit into a school-level system, and to follow up on the intervention plans crafted to meet their demonstrated needs. Along the way of building an RTI model, we listen in on the challenges and solutions encountered by school staff and students as they work for better outcomes for these individual students.

SUGGESTED RESOURCES TO SUPPORT RTI
IMPLEMENTATION AT YOUR SCHOOL

Johnson, E., Mellard, D. F., Fuchs, D., & McKnight, M. A. (2006). *Responsiveness to intervention (RTI): How to do it.* Lawrence, KS: National Research Center on Learning Disabilities. Available for free at *www.nrcld.org*.

Mellard, D. F., & Johnson, D. F. (2008). *RTI: A practitioners guide to implementing response to intervention.* Thousand Oaks, CA: Corwin Press.

These are two very useful resources in creating a road map to support RTI implementation. The first is available to download for free on the National Research Council for Learning Disabilities website. The second features much of the same information in a book. They are accessible and include checklists to help a school engage in the implementation of each component of an RTI model, suggesting this should be done step-by-step and in phases. The website also includes case studies to demonstrate the ways that schools have approached RTI implementation.

From a Comprehensive Assessment Battery to a Systematic RTI Model

At Rosa Parks Elementary, as with any school that serves a number of students who encounter difficulties on their way to developing academic literacy, an assessment battery serves many functions. Because of the multidimensional nature of understanding literacy development, rolling out an RTI model is far more than a single-step process. Indeed, RTI is best thought of as a collection of practices that, when combined, provide differentiated instruction to meet each student's needs. As we think about this implementation, there are a number of characteristics of an RTI system that work in practice (Shapiro, Zigmond, Wallace, & Marston, 2011). In this chapter, we unpack what we think of as three crucial hallmarks:

1. Comprehensive, continual screening of developing literacy skills.
2. Data systems that make scores clear and accessible for translating to practice.
3. Detailed plans and specialized practices to respond to student needs.

Once these structural pieces are in place, it is far easier to realize the potential of a good RTI system. That is, an instructional core differentiated to reflect the pattern of students' needs that surface in the data, as well as targeted intervention for students whose needs are not otherwise being met by the core curriculum.

We are going to walk through just how Rosa Parks Elementary arrived at an RTI system characterized by each of these three hallmarks; in so doing, we have our profile students in mind. For example, in discussing the first hallmark, we see how Carter fits into a schoolwide screening system. In discussing the second, we see how Marcia's teacher aptly placed her performance in context of her peers and restructured the reading block accordingly. Finally, we close with two students with special needs (Max and Kim) who highlight the vital role of collaboration of specialists, teachers, and families if the RTI model is to be effective. We begin with the first hallmark.

Comprehensive, Continual Screening of Developing Literacy Skills

In Chapter 3 we make a case for why schools need to screen all students on key domains of literacy skills in order to identify potential problems and gain an understanding of collective needs. That said, literacy skills require a different tactic for screening than many other areas of development. For example, we can screen a child for hearing and vision difficulties when he or she enters kindergarten (or preschool) and may not need to follow up for several years. Literacy development, in contrast, is far more dynamic. Even when discussing the five skill areas identified by the National Reading Panel (National Institute of Child Health and Human Development, 2000), we cannot blindly apply these to all elementary students. Kindergarteners generally have not been reading long enough to participate in measures of text reading fluency; in contrast, phonological awareness is generally established by first grade, and there is little evidence to suggest it is useful to provide direct instruction after first grade in a regular education setting (Snow et al., 1998). Therefore, we would not screen kindergarteners using a measure of passage fluency, nor would we screen third graders using a measure of phonological awareness.

To complicate matters, each domain develops at a different pace, as a function of whether they can be "mastered" or not. Some skills are universally mastered in a relatively brief period of time; they are skills that are typically learned quickly with appropriate instruction and are not a lasting source of individual differences in reading ability for the great majority of students (Paris, 2005). Phonics is a good example here: there are 26 letters, 44 sounds, and a number of resulting combinations. These skills are firmly established by strong readers at age 6 or 7. In contrast, other skills or competencies, especially those in the meaning-related domain, do not lend themselves to mastery. In fact, some elements of literacy develop relatively steadily across the lifetime. They cannot be taught in a relatively brief period of time and instead must be developed over many years. Many of these skills and competencies, particularly vocabulary knowledge (by which we effectively mean background knowledge), are key sources of lasting differences in individuals' reading ability.

These differences with respect to mastery and the time frame for development have implications for how we think about our screening system. Throughout the time period during which those mastery-oriented skills should be developing rapidly, we want to screen regularly—twice or even three times yearly. It's the only way to ensure that students are on track and to intervene promptly with those who aren't progressing at a rate that will keep them on grade level.

For example, a first grader should double his or her passage reading fluency (i.e., WCPM) between the middle and the end of the year. Screening only once would not be sufficient to capture development in such a rapidly evolving skill. In comparison, we might be able to screen for meaning-related difficulties only once or twice per year.

Given this need to determine an appropriate screening schedule, the leadership team at Rosa Parks Elementary generated the contents of Table 7.1, outlining what assessments were to be given, at what intervals, and by grade level, across the school. A first grader like Kim would be monitored on phonological awareness and phonics in the fall, winter, and spring, adding in a fluency measure in the winter. A second grader like Max would be screened on fluency for these three time periods, and phonics once; those students who did not perform at benchmark on phonics would receive additional screening in the winter and, if applicable, spring. Similarly, for fourth and fifth graders like Carter and Marcia, respectively, there would also be a quick phonics screener in the fall with fluency assessments at all three intervals. All these students, regardless of age, would receive some measure of text comprehension (oral/listening instead of reading for kindergarteners) in the fall and spring. And all students would also participate in a spring administration of a vocabulary screening, with follow-up mid-fall for students below benchmark. Of course, in some ways, this table reflects local needs; school staff will consider some of the strengths and weaknesses of their student population in constructing the table. Nevertheless, the information in Table 7.1 represents a general schedule for assessment, in light of the different pace at which domains of literacy develop.

As you look at Table 7.1, it can be helpful to think about vertical alignment of an assessment battery. In Chapter 2 we discuss the importance of having at least two measures that are the same from year to year: one in code-based

TABLE 7.1. Rosa Parks Elementary's Assessment Plan

Grade level	Phonological awareness	Phonics	Fluency	Vocabulary	Text comprehension
Preschool	Emergent	Emergent	Not applicable	Developing	Emerging listening comprehension skills
Kindergarten	Developing	Emergent/developing	Not applicable	Developing	Developing listening comprehension skills
First grade	Developing/established	Developing	Emerging	Developing	Developing listening comprehension skills/emerging text comprehension skills
Second grade	Established	Developing	Developing	Developing	Developing
Third grade	Established	Developing/established	Developing	Developing	Developing
Fourth grade	Established	Established	Developing	Developing	Developing
Fifth grade	Established	Established	Developing	Developing	Developing
Testing decision	Screen at least twice per year through kindergarten; once in first grade, with an additional screening period for first graders not established; discontinue past first grade.	Screen at least twice per year through second grade; screen once per year in third through fifth grade with additional screening period for those not established.	Screen beginning in the winter of first grade, and at least twice per year in second through fifth grade.	Screen at least once per year in all grades; additional screening period for those with low scores.	Screen at least twice per year in kindergarten through fifth grade. Focus preschool efforts on measure of oral language instead.

WHO ADMINISTERS THE ASSESSMENTS?

In planning for an effective RTI model, an important question to be answered is: *Who will administer the assessments?* For any progress monitoring assessment, it is important to have the student's teacher engaged in the assessment process. After all, it is the *process* of observing students engaged in literacy-related tasks that provides rich information to drive instruction, and formative assessments can often be built into the instructional day. In sharp contrast, there is no specific reason for teachers to be involved in the administration of screening and outcome assessments.

Why are we not advocating for teachers to be directly and/or heavily involved in the administration of screening and outcome assessments? Well, the testing scenario is not meant to be authentic or "in context," and the tasks themselves are at an arm's length from instructional practice. In order to provide rich instruction in the skill of interest, teachers will need to determine best practice in a given area rather than, for example, correct errors made during the assessment, or, worse, replicate testing procedures in class. Ultimately, this means that the efficient administration of screening and outcome assessments focuses on maximizing teachers' time on their most important role: teaching.

At Rosa Parks Elementary, Margarita and Principal Lansdowne worked together to determine the best strategy for test administration. With input from teachers, they identified the vocabulary screening assessments as particularly time consuming; moreover, they all agreed it was the results—not the testing procedure—that were crucial to understanding student literacy development. The vocabulary assessments were administered by a special testing team that included the school counselor, the speech–language pathologist, and two teachers who had been previously trained in the measure when the district had used it years before. With no interruptions, it took each team member about a day per classroom, sometimes only the morning in the younger classrooms. They generally set up in the hallway directly outside of the class, as described at the beginning of the chapter, alphabetically moving down the list of student names. Sometimes a parent volunteer helped the counselor shepherd students to and from class to testing so that it could be done in her office. This process generally took a week, with Margarita following up with students who managed to miss the regular and makeup sessions, or who did not have a good test day for whatever reason. The testing team included all students at the school in the spring, with follow-up in October by Margarita only for students with low scores. In the long run, this reduced the amount of time teachers had been spending on assessments from about 20 minutes per student before changing their battery (see Chapter 1) to about 10 minutes or less per student, since teachers still administered the classwide text comprehension measure and the code-based measures. Ultimately, teachers had more time for instruction after the school reshaped its literacy battery.

skills and the other in meaning-related skills. Having consistency in these scores will give a better understanding of students' literacy trajectories while promoting a common dialogue among school staff. As we've previously discussed and will discuss again here, following students from year to year is especially important in responding quickly to demonstrated needs; otherwise, each year might require a waiting period to turn up needs, then determine if these difficulties are persistent. We can understand how well a student is responding to instruction if we have some consistency in scoring measures over time.

Revisiting Carter: The Benefits of Continual Screening

So how did this screening model play out for a student like Carter? When he participated in a winter administration of the screening battery, he scored above benchmark in fluency, but well below benchmark in vocabulary and text comprehension. To his fourth-grade teacher, Franny Bartek, Carter was a bit unusual in that his low scores in vocabulary and text comprehension contrasted so sharply with his advanced word-reading skills. However, with the results of screening measures available from all students, it became clear that his performance was actually in sync with an overall pattern in her group of fourth graders. Carter's relative ease with word-level skills coupled with considerable difficulties around academic language and text comprehension was not unique; while his profile was more striking, many of his peers had similarly underdeveloped language and comprehension skills. Indeed, this profile was common among all fourth graders, not just those in Franny's room.

The fact that most fourth graders at Rosa Parks Elementary had low vocabulary scores signaled the need to adapt the core of instruction, system-wide. Vocabulary and meaning-related instruction would need to become intensified across the core so that it could serve as an intervention, of sorts, for fourth graders like Carter, and ultimately bolster these skills for all students. In fact, a language-, content,- and text-rich learning environment is what Carter and his peers need. Unlike code-based difficulties, supporting vocabulary and comprehension development is best accomplished when bolstered throughout the day, and certainly throughout the literacy block. The fourth-grade team united around a common goal of identifying an appropriate number of words for intentional, explicit vocabulary instruction. After discussing what this might look like, they decided that the words and teaching recommendations that came with their core reading curriculum were not sufficient—it was not the story words that were tripping up Carter and his peers. As a result, they decided to supplement this instruction with academic vocabulary instruction, using words drawn from texts across the content areas.

"Enough with the historical fiction!" declared one of Franny's colleagues at a planning meeting, as the group of fourth-grade teachers at Rosa Parks Elementary discussed potential themes. "How are we going to start engaging our boys with text?" As the group brainstormed ideas for bringing in more informational text, the suggestion of baseball drew support. The big idea for the unit would be population and resource distribution, focusing on the players' stories and where they came from before making it to the big leagues. The unit would coincide with the season opener, and along with the social studies content would bring in math (percentages), science (weather), and reading (biographies, newspaper and magazine articles). Students would each choose a current or former player and write a five-paragraph report on who he was, where he came from, and where he moved in his baseball career, as well as showing highlights of the player's stats.

The teachers split up the unit into weeks, each of them responsible for 1 week's worth of lesson planning around vocabulary instruction. Based on information they had at hand, they decided that students would at least need to hear the words, get kid-friendly definitions, and use the words in their extended writing in order to build sufficient understanding of their meanings. Meanwhile, the teachers would work to connect the words to real-life examples while also structuring thematically related discussions and debates in which students would practice using these words. The last day of each week would be devoted to writing that incorporated the use of the target vocabulary words, requiring students to extend their word knowledge from speech to writing. Throughout the unit, teachers would continuously monitor progress using tests they generated, looking at students' written work, and carefully listening to students' answers during group discussion and collaborative learning activities.

As it turned out, Carter loved the baseball unit, but this did not put Franny's mind at ease. While he made steady progress with words that were explicitly taught, as evidenced by diagnostic assessments, he still struggled with understanding much of the text given to him. Rather than welcoming the informational text, Carter was initially confused by the different features and structures of this less familiar genre. Several weeks passed before he self-selected to read biographies, although he did quite well with magazine articles on his favorite players. When the final round of screening assessments were given that spring, Carter showed some small progress in text comprehension,

WHAT ABOUT COMPUTER-BASED SCREENING AND ASSESSMENT?

Computer-based assessments provide one possible route toward fast and efficient screening of student skills. However, there are some elements of computer-based assessments that require careful attention before investing time and money. First, building any effective assessment battery requires establishing a clear purpose for assessment. Just like the manual assessment, any computer-based test is likely to just do *one* thing well. Being electronic likely does not make it any more sophisticated or comprehensive. Second, we would argue that computers should be used sparingly, if at all, for diagnostic purposes. Good diagnostic assessment engages teachers in careful observation of students working through meaningful literacy tasks. Most importantly, as with our manual assessments, it is imperative that computer-based scores be put to good use. We have encountered schools where students are involved in computer-based assessments, but the many scores they generate are given minimal scrutiny. Sometimes these computer-based assessments begin to feel like a classroom center in their own right because students are so often at the computer taking one test or another. If this is the case—and scores are not being put to good use—there are certainly better alternatives for integrating technology into literacy than through assessment. For example, students might participate in a computer-based program that rewards students with points for answering questions on a text they have read, thus providing incentives for students to go back to the class library and pick up another book to read for meaning.

but had the same percentile rank score in vocabulary. "We have to remember that most other 9-year-olds are learning lots of new words, too," counseled Margarita, who pointed out that maintaining the same rate of growth, as opposed to losing ground, was not necessarily a loss—in fact, it was somewhat promising in a dynamic area like vocabulary. Still, Carter's issues, much like the majority of his peers, were far from resolved. Both Carter and his classmates would continue to need explicit instruction in vocabulary and text comprehension.

In order to ensure that the momentum captured in the spring of fourth grade would continue into the final year of elementary school, good data needed to be coupled with good data-sharing systems so that the fifth-grade teachers could immediately understand the needs of their new cohort. In the next section, we turn to the importance of data storing and sharing systems.

We turn now to the second hallmark of an effective RTI system, focused on data systems.

Creating Data Systems That Make Scores Clear and Accessible for Translating to Practice

As soon as all test administration is complete, it is important to have one common, centralized location for reporting scores. Not only does this create the potential for shared language around assessment and results, the common system creates a bridge from year to year for understanding student performance. We recommend creating a database where scores from all different assessments can be compiled side-by-side, making it easy to see relative areas of strength and weakness for individuals, classrooms, grade levels, and even the school population at large. These days several assessments come packaged with advanced software options, including databases that generate detailed score reports. However, problems arise when different tests have different software systems that do not connect. School leaders and teachers are then left with disparate data, and must look back and forth in order to understand the overall instructional profile of their students.

The system we have used with the most success—and is in use at Rosa Parks Elementary— is a simple electronic spreadsheet stored on a secure, shared drive with a separate "sheet" for every classroom or grade level. Margarita, who had only moderate computing skills, formatted the workbook so that cells are automatically color coded based on the value of the scores that are entered. It's a matter of setting threshold numbers for "high-risk," "some-risk," and "low-risk" scores, and such that cell values within these ranges will automatically turn red, yellow, and green, respectively. Once the table is formatted, school staff members enter results into this shared workbook, thus automatically generating a color-coded table where students' instructional needs are highlighted and visible across the school. The next year, students' scores can be cut and pasted into a new spreadsheet, providing an easy-to-access archive of their developmental trajectory in literacy. In addition, spreadsheets and workbooks can easily generate various tables and charts (see Chapter 6, Figure 6.2, for one example of a helpful graph), as well as "sort" students from lowest to highest scores. In a school climate that is sensitive to others viewing scores, it is possible to set up a password-protected workbook for each teacher on a shared drive that is still viewable by school leaders.

As part of the testing calendar, dates for scoring and reporting are essential (discussed in greater detail in Chapter 8). At Rosa Parks Elementary, meetings to discuss results were held as soon as possible after the turnaround deadline, usually within 10 days. Teachers came to these meetings equipped with an organized and straightforward table of student scores and a graph summarizing the key areas of strength and weakness. We have found it useful for teachers to meet in grade-level teams to share and discuss their findings from these combined score reports. Very often the areas of greatest need are shared across classrooms, opening up dialogue on how best to support these areas in a manner specific to that particular age and set of curricular materials. In these initial meetings, the color- (or symbol-) coded tables and charts help focus participants on the task at hand: to talk about instructional needs at a classroom level.

Following Up with Marcia: The Role of Good Score-Reporting Systems

The importance of clear data is perhaps best displayed with Marcia, an ELL student (no longer formally classified as such) who had been enrolled at Rosa Parks Elementary since kindergarten. She had long since passed the level of oral proficiency set for supported instruction, but nonetheless experienced academic difficulties in the upper elementary years. Her teacher, Bob Thompson, was not sure about the role her language skills played in her difficulties, and whether she could (or should) fit into general instruction. A bit of a spreadsheet buff, Bob had used the worksheet for his classroom to look at results in numerous ways, certain he would find trends in how students were performing. He had added columns to identify student race, gender, and home language, and had used these identifiers to sort results, looking for the best way to group students (for instance, Marcia) for instruction.

The results he had to share with his colleagues, however, surprised him. Nearly half of his students were flagged as having a low vocabulary, but there was considerable diversity among the group of students with the lowest scores. It certainly included students, like Marcia, who spoke a language other than English at home. However, there were plenty of native-English speakers with low vocabularies. Moreover, he had two students who had immigrated to the United States and since kindergarten scored in the normal range. Another student who arrived from Ghana just 2 years before had a low score, but far from the lowest in the classroom, and quite a bit higher than what Bob expected. "What I am seeing," he said at the opening of the meeting, "is that vocabulary is a big need in my classroom, but not in the way I thought it would be. There are no stark divisions between who speaks what language and who needs help with vocabulary."

That said, the results of the screening assessment were of concern to Bob as well as his colleagues. Bob felt it was clear that Marcia did, after all, fit in with the majority of fifth graders, who clearly needed an enriched print and language environment in the classroom. Not only did half of the fifth-grade class have low vocabulary, close to 70% did not meet the benchmark for text comprehension. However, this group of teachers was divided on the best approach to meeting those needs. "Here's the thing," said one teacher, "next year they go to middle school. There will be a science teacher, a math teacher, and on and on. If all I teach for the rest of the year is vocabulary and reading, how is that going to prepare them to go into those classes? Sure, reading is an area with a lot of need, but have you looked at math scores lately?"

After some conversation about improving reading without sacrificing other subjects, the group decided that a strong and appropriate focus was classroom discussion. By promoting classroom discussion, they could build language across different parts of the day, particularly the content-rich areas of science and social studies. This would also help build the ELLs' language skills. Indeed, research shows that rich classroom discussions support reading comprehension (see Murphy, Wilkinson, Soter, Hennessey, & Alexander, 2009).

Margarita took a two-pronged approach to supporting the fifth-grade teachers. First, she led a discussion about continuing the work of the fourth-grade teachers in the next year, as the rising students would benefit from a spiraled focus on vocabulary along with language development. Second, she checked in with the district literacy coordinators and found out that many middle school teachers were involved in a book study about deepening discussions around different content. Margarita secured enough copies for her fifth-grade team. Through this text (*Content Area Conversations;* Fisher, Frey, & Rothenberg, 2008), Bob began to develop language goals along with content goals, as well as instituting several structured discussion activities that became part of the common routines in the classroom day.

This new focus on discussion was certainly outside of Marcia's comfort level. Quiet and shy, she was not one to jump into classroom discussions. Bob had allowed Marcia to sit out of classroom discussions before as he was sensitive to her introverted nature, and was uncertain how her status as an ELL student affected her when it came to speaking. However, he adopted the structured discussion activities outlined in the book he was studying to ensure that she had time to think, share with a small group, and prepare a response before possibly being called on to talk in front of the class. At the suggestion of the authors, he also provided language frames, structured sentence stems like:

The things they have in common are _____.

A distinction between _____ and _____ might be _____.

They are similar because_____.

to promote speaking skills and active participation. While Marcia did not volunteer more in class, these new routines required a sharp increase in her class participation, and Marcia was, in fact, able to join the dialogue. Areas of confusion began to surface (like when Marcia thought that a character was "perceptive" because she could see well and did not need glasses), allowing Bob to become far more responsive to her needs.

As time went on, Marcia's answers became more complete and showed better understanding of how to structure responses along with a deeper engagement with content. These improvements were also reflected in her writing. Much as they had with Carter, however, the spring round of screening assessments revealed that Marcia was still below the target range in vocabulary and text comprehension. It would be up to her middle school teachers to provide continued support as she moved forward in her academic career. Bob hoped that she would encounter many of the same discussion activities in middle school as she had participated in during fifth grade, perhaps giving her some confidence as she transitioned to this new phase.

While there are many students like Carter and Marcia whose needs are far from unique in their classrooms, there are certainly others who display individualized needs—needs that aren't necessarily reflected in the trends. While the initial thrust for any schoolwide testing period needs to focus on the instructional core in order to ensure that students have a strong base of learning upon which to build, we also need systems for those students, like Max and Kim, who require specialized intervention. That is the third hallmark of an effective RTI system that we address in this book.

Detailed Plans and Specialized Practices to Respond to Student Needs

A guiding principle of RTI is to provide students with instructional opportunities closely aligned to their demonstrated needs; when problems persist, these efforts are intensified. Again, a vertically aligned assessment battery helps us identify whether students continue to struggle from year to year. For example, if in the fall of second grade a student's score on a phonics screener suggests a "red light" or "warning," we can quickly tell whether these difficulties were present in first grade. We are going to be particularly concerned about low scores if classmates' weaknesses or problems have resolved. We note that if a student is new to a school because of transfer status, immigration status, or just because he or she is young and entering school for the first time, and arrives following a testing window, we would want to provide the opportunity to respond to instruction before beginning additional tiers of intervention. After all, a strong core of instruction is already an intervention and is, in fact, the first level of differentiation (see Chapter 6).

Once students with persistent difficulties are identified, a plan needs to be instituted for either individual or small-group intervention. These students will also need to be monitored closely to ensure that the intervention is, in fact, meeting their needs. As discussed in depth in Chapter 4, progress monitoring assessments guide us in understanding whether students are continually demonstrating improvement and inform our midcourse corrections if this is not the case. At Rosa Parks Elementary, these more frequent assessments were also built into the calendar as part of the new RTI model. If the model was to be effective, those students requiring additional instructional supports would participate in monthly progress monitoring assessments. Special grade-level team meetings were scheduled for the first week of the month, with the clear expectation that teachers would bring copies of progress monitoring measures along with student work and results on probes (diagnostic measures) for a student with individualized needs, with time allocated on the agenda for each teacher. The meeting would involve discussing strategies around intervention and monitoring and documenting progress (or lack thereof).

A comprehensive RTI model includes a schedule for progress monitoring assessments to be administered. However, there is also a need to use diagnostic measures to identify the source of difficulties and continuously tailor instruction to the student's needs and interests. And truly undertaking diagnostic assessment requires a *mindset*—one that is really about the importance of carefully observing student work. In fact, there is not always a need to purchase testing kits for the purpose of diagnostics. Margarita, the literacy coordinator at Rosa Parks Elementary whom we met at the outset of this chapter, elicited ideas from teachers as to how they monitored and observed students. She then created an inventory with ideas for different areas of literacy, shown in Table 7.2. This mindset of careful observation is not always easy to foster, and there were certainly times at Rosa Parks Elementary that diagnostic assessments were administered strictly to "meet requirements" rather than to deeply understand student performance. In these cases—where it's clear that more staff development is needed—it may be particularly helpful to use published diagnostic assessments that guide teachers through a process of formal observation and analysis, such as Marie Clay's Observation Survey or the Developmental Reading Assessment.

At the school level, systems need to be in place in order to ensure effective supplementary supports, but there is also a need for systems that provide

TABLE 7.2. Diagnostic Assessment in the Classroom

Area	Ideas for diagnostic assessment through observation
Phonological awareness	Rhymes, songs, cloze activities (e.g., "Jack and Jill went up the _____"), clapping for each sound in the word, representing word sounds as blocks, listening to a word and picking which of two sounds is heard in the word
Phonics	Running record with analysis of miscues, word games, spelling tests, writing samples
Fluency	Running record with calculation of words read correctly per minute, charting the time it took for the student(s) to complete a passage, as well as errors and self-corrections. The degree of prosody (i.e., expression and phrasing) is noted using a rubric or rating scale, or just recorded in notes
Vocabulary	Asking students to use a new word in a sentence (written or spoken), classifying words, making visual representations of words, changing a word's form (e.g., *observe* → *observer*), writing samples, analogies
Text comprehension	Graphic organizers, story retells, story discussions, think-alouds, quizzes and story tests, reading notebooks

further evaluation of those students who do not respond to classroom-based supplementary supports. Typically, schools have some sort of student support process whereby teachers refer struggling students to the team, resulting in a multidisciplinary team meeting focused on responding to the students' needs. Recall that in Chapter 4 (see Figure 4.4), we included a detailed decision tree designed to guide decisions around whether it is appropriate to refer a student to the student support team.

Following Up with Max: Providing Additional Tiers of Instruction

Second-grade teacher Pam Perez had been working closely with Max all year. The shy, sweet little boy had been part of daily reading groups, both with her and a volunteer tutor who worked with select students in the school. There was ample record of his unusual struggles with reading, from his earliest days at school. When Pam received the results from the midyear testing cycle, and went through the routine steps of understanding his individual profile as a learner (see Chapter 4), she realized that she should provide even more strategic supplemental instruction. These midcourse corrections refocused his code-based skills instruction more specifically to his demonstrated needs while finding avenues to strengthen his meaning-related skills through read-alouds and listening centers.

After several weeks of careful tutoring, Pam saw some improvement in Max's performance, particularly on code-based skills and the specific exercises that were part of tutoring. She was concerned, however, that she was not seeing his skills translate to his book reading. After discussing his work with her colleagues at one of the monthly scheduled meetings described above, Pam referred Max to the student support team—not necessarily for the purposes of identification at this point, but for a support plan to take him through to the end of second grade. Pam wanted additional input from specialists and reassurance that efforts to support his reading were coordinated.

With his parents, the literacy coordinator, and an inclusion specialist at the meeting, Pam shared her detailed notes and samples of Max's work along with his test scores. The group put their heads together to generate the best possible instructional plan for Max, both at home and at school. His parents agreed to have Max read a short selected passage three times per night to help build fluency, and also to reinstate their old routine of reading aloud to him, this time with chapter books of his choosing (they had previously stopped this practice, thinking it was more important to have Max practice reading words than to hear stories). At school, Max would continue with tutoring, which would be expanded on in a special afterschool program that could potentially be continued into the summer. In addition, Max would have increased exposure to text through listening centers. In particular, Pam would dust off the audio recordings that came packaged with the social studies and science texts. At home, his parents could have him listening to books on an iPod, or listening to interesting podcasts to keep him learning. Together, the group agreed that the best strategy now, and probably going forward, was to keep him "in print"—building up his knowledge and love for learning—without always having him decoding print. Many children like Max fall behind in their overall literacy development because their laborious decoding means they read less, overall, and because they can't easily handle sophisticated text. Fortunately, with today's technology, keeping Max in print without having him doing the reading is easily achievable.

After the meeting, Pam had a long conversation with Max's parents. She was not surprised to learn that Max's father had also struggled with reading; his mom expressed concern that their family schedule of late—leaving less time for Max's reading—had perhaps exacerbated Max's difficulties. Pam often felt a bit uncertain speaking with parents—she had no children of her own yet, and often felt like she was unqualified to offer ideas on parenting. However, she reassured Max's mother that his reading difficulties were more than likely unavoidable. "Some children just have a hard time learning to read," Pam said. "We can help him with this."

The next day, Pam invited Max to a special lunch with just her in the classroom. She resisted the urge to pull out his workbook and texts, to use this as another opportunity to build his skills. She saw in front of her a little boy touched by the special attention. That day, she focused on learning more about Max: his interests, his likes and dislikes, and how he felt about second grade. She shared with Margarita that one of her greatest lessons from working with Max was to keep the individual in mind first. "I think we have a good plan in place for him in terms of reading," she said. "I want to make sure that I still see him as a whole person, with a multitude of strengths. Reading is important, but it isn't everything. More than anything, I want to have a good connection with him."

Following Up with Kim: Formal Evaluation and Educational Planning

Down the hall from Max, in the first-grade classroom, Kim had already been evaluated by the special education department of Rosa Parks Elementary. The results indicated that Kim qualified as having a gifted exceptionality and should receive special services. At the IEP meeting, the gifted and talented coordinator for the district, Rosa Park's inclusion specialist, Sharona Jackson (Kim's classroom teacher), Principal Lansdowne, and Kim's parents sat down together to discuss her educational needs.

Kim was going to receive some pull-out services: once a week she would leave her classroom to join a group of students schoolwide who met with the gifted and talented program coordinator. During this time she would be challenged to complete projects that required creativity and advanced problem-solving skills. In addition, a major focus of the gifted and talented program was to help students self-monitor their own behavior in their regular classroom settings. What could she do if she were bored? Finished early? How could she respond to others appropriately if she knew more on a subject? Much in the same way that Marcia benefited from linguistic frames to enter classroom conversations, Kim benefited from sentence stems (or linguistic frames) to help her respond in a friendly manner to classmates. These were practiced regularly in the gifted and talented program during role play that involved everyday social scenarios in the classroom and on the playground.

The IEP team also discussed plans for regular classroom instruction. Of note was the formulaic nature of Kim's beloved series. While these books were a fine choice for recreational reading, they did not represent enough challenge for classroom time. Kim would be tasked with leading a literature circle on books with more advanced themes—a title by Patricia Polacco was an initial pick, but she would then be required to read an informational book for every fiction book thereafter. As part of Kim's homework, she would think of and write one to three questions she could ask her group after they partner read the selection the next day.

Kim was, indeed, challenged by the new text she was assigned. She worked closely with her parents to come up with questions at home, leading to deep discussions of the text, but also how to include some of her peers in her own excitement for reading. Kim did not always like the books she was asked to read, and found some of the informational books quite difficult. Indeed, some of her classmates outperformed her on topics of their interest, like dinosaurs. Kim was still unique because she went to the second-grade classroom for reading and the resource room once a week, but she became a more and more normal part of Sharona's first-grade classroom. Her dramatic pronouncements of boredom were met with a quiet question: "So what will you do now?" And with this prompting, Kim would determine an appropriate course of action.

The resource teacher at Rosa Parks Elementary who worked with students like Kim discussed with the team that down the line, Kim may struggle with reading comprehension on account of her social difficulties; much of the meaning-making process with sophisticated text, especially narrative text, requires a significant amount of perspective taking and proficiency with social cues. Although currently a strong reader at first grade, Kim had a very literal style to her. In this meeting, the second-grade teacher who hosted Kim in the weekly reading group meeting commented that inference making and literary tools, like similes and plays on words, in books at her grade level were beginning to be somewhat lost on her. For these reasons, it made sense that unlocking the social side of text and language may well be a part of their support plan for the years to come.

The Nuts and Bolts, and Beyond

In this chapter, we focused on some of the key structural issues to consider when implementing a schoolwide RTI model. Getting the nuts and bolts into place is, indeed, crucial. As you finish this chapter, you will want to consider how close your school is to a true RTI model. Do you have a comprehensive assessment battery in place? Are students systematically screened and then monitored over time? Is there a system in place to combine scores and make them easily accessible to teachers and instructional leaders? How do you ensure that all children receiving supplemental instruction are carefully monitored over time? Each of these is one piece of a larger goal toward strong literacy instruction.

But beyond the nuts and bolts, and inherent in getting these secured tightly into place, lies the challenge of leading the change. This includes, but is not limited to, the habits of mind, the persistence, and the knowledge building necessary to translate good structures into good practice. After all, we've all seen carefully mapped out reform efforts fail to gain enough traction to really drive change. In some cases they might get off to a great start, but not survive the summer vacation and the next set of initiatives introduced that fall. In others, it may be that only a small group of leaders and staff are focused on implementation. In other cases, while all may be introduced to the plan, teachers are not provided with enough (ongoing) support that results in the knowledge and practice needed to change their instruction. Whatever the reason, under these reform circumstances we never really do justice to Carter, Max, Kim, Marcia, and all of their peers, who depend upon our coordinated, effective, and deeply sustained efforts for academic success. So, our next and final chapter focuses on the challenges, key steps, and rewards of leading change that results in genuine data-driven instruction.

CHAPTER 8

Leading Data-Driven Instruction

To Principal Lansdowne it hardly seemed possible that the school year was drawing to a close despite the clear evidence: the classroom field trips, jubilant voices on the playground on warm afternoons, and the flurry of meetings to coordinate fifth-grade graduation. She suspected everyone looked forward to this final stretch of the school year when the state accountability tests were completed. It was almost as if, across the building, there was a collective sigh of relief; teachers were eager to pursue more fun and relaxed learning activities. The promise of summer vacation beckoned pleasantly—the finish line was in sight.

Every spring, Principal Lansdowne felt determined to capture this last gust of energy to channel toward planning for the next year. But her good intentions were so often foiled by the endless administrative tasks required before the academic year wound up. Today, for example, just as she was reaching for the large binder on her crowded desk, she realized she first needed to process behavior referrals. Within that binder, though, the spring assessment results from each class were recorded, neatly sectioned off by grade level and classroom with dividers. She had barely the time to glance them over, and doubted her teachers had done more than check to see whether their students showed growth. This troubled her. Hopefully they hadn't worked so hard to get together a new assessment battery only to return to status quo—letting data and reports accumulate on a shelf (or an overflowing desk).

Once again Principal Lansdowne renewed her dedication to instructional planning. Indeed, as she looked toward the year ahead, she desperately wanted a strategy to ensure that the new literacy battery meant instructional improvement. She knew that she couldn't expect teachers to embrace this new assessment strategy with enthusiasm or implement it with high fidelity and sufficient intensity unless she provided the necessary training and ongoing support. She also understood that the assessment strategy's central role in instructional conversations and initiatives at Rosa Parks Elementary, including team meetings and professional development sessions, would have to be communicated clearly. Importantly, she needs to effectively recruit and engage her teachers, instructional leaders, and staff in this process—without them, change is impossible.

Beyond logistics, translating scores into differentiated, student-centered instruction is hard work; implementing good data-driven literacy assessment at the school and district levels is a complex problem for which there are no easy answers. But, there are certainly processes we can use to guide us in a positive direction. In this chapter we discuss leading data-driven instruction. We share the process that we have used with instructional leaders—including district leaders, school-based administrators, and literacy coaches—to create and maintain a focus on providing a cohesive approach to literacy instruction within schools and districts, using data as a road map. In doing so, we attend to both the logistical issues of data collection and score analysis, and those related to leading and managing adults through a change process.

We delineate a two-pronged approach to leading this change. First, we focus on creating an assessment strategy that is purpose driven and works in the service of the larger mission of the organization. Second, we lay out a plan for analyzing and discussing data throughout the year that is coordinated to promote common goals among the school staff. This plan begins by focusing the whole school on a common instructional priority that can be bolstered by prescheduled, routine grade-level and vertical team meetings with a set agenda. With careful planning and attention to leading change in an organization, data-driven instruction can be woven into the fabric of the school year, rather than end up as a fad to be weathered.

Step 1: Crafting an Assessment Strategy

Effecting change in instructional practice and student achievement is challenging. Yet, we cannot expect improvement if we continue with the same approaches or jump from initiative to initiative without clear data pointing out the direction, hoping that the new major fad happens to correspond with our students' needs. Crafting an assessment strategy helps keep our work on track by focusing staff on clear and compelling goals, and helps to support full implementation of the new approach to assessment-based instruction.

Putting a Team Together (for More Than a Year)

To begin crafting a strategy, we advise first bringing together key players—generate a team and call it what makes the most sense for your building: a leadership team, data team, a strategic improvement team, and so on. The name, however, is not nearly as important as the composition of the team—members should be diverse (however you define it) and respected by their peers. They should be "nodes" in the professional network of the building, and the process of deciding who is on the team must be perceived as fair and transparent. One possible team composition is a teacher from every grade level, a parent, and a few supporting staff members. In our work, we've suggested that when these teams are formed, they are to last 2 years. This 2-year conceptualization and commitment is helpful for two reasons: it dispels the response that this is *yet another* initiative—the flavor of the year, so to speak, and it recognizes that more than a year is needed to get things well off the ground. In fact, it takes a sustained effort over many years, but ongoing work over 2 years with a key group of people is a very good start. One thing is for sure: a year is not nearly enough to gain sufficient traction.

Creating a Purpose Statement

Once formed, we suggest that the team's first task is to create a purpose statement for assessment, guided by some questions: Why are we using assessments? What do we hope for in using assessments? How do we intend to use the results? What do you find most useful about assessments, in principle or in practice? The *process* of putting together a purpose statement is often more important than the statement itself; it raises awareness and reminds all about the role(s) of assessment, creates buy-in, and makes everyone own the next steps. It's an excellent way to bring focus to the 2-year task at hand and, actually, to begin to bring together an otherwise disparate group of people—they may work in the same building but they may not interface much, they may be guided by different causes, readers, and interests—and to ensure everyone is on the same page. In this process, beliefs and challenges will bubble up, and important conversations will ensue. For example, the core challenge for Principal Lansdowne's leadership team lies in identifying what they were trying to accomplish in testing their students. As a first step in strengthening the link between assessment and instruction, the principal and her team drafted a purpose statement for their literacy battery that was aligned with the school's overall mission statement. They wanted to share some core values that everyone in the school could agree were important and that provided clarity on why assessments were given and how they were to be used. The ideal purpose statement, they realized, could be shared with families as well as staff, as part of a living document, disseminated every year. Here is what they wrote:

> At Rosa Parks Elementary, we believe very seriously in student assessment. The better we understand our students, the better the instruction we will provide. We believe that data-driven instruction has great potential to increase achievement, prevent social and academic difficulties, and will ultimately help our students reach their greatest potential as caring, productive citizens. Data-driven instruction is anchored by *comprehensive screening and progress monitoring* of students as readers. As part of our assessment system, we use several assessments because different assessment tools have different capabilities and serve different purposes; also, we use some of the same assessments from year to year to understand/follow our readers over time. No one assessment is sufficient to screen for early difficulties or monitor progress in the many skills that go into literacy success.

Aligning Current Assessment Practices with the Purpose Statement

The process of putting together a purpose statement was the team's first step. Once it was established that the school wanted a comprehensive screening and progress monitoring battery, it became clear that their old approach to assessment—getting just one global reading score for each student—was no longer sufficient. Therefore, the team's next step was to select testing tools aligned with their new, collective purpose. Once new testing tools were selected (see Chapter 3), the leadership team spent some time writing a description of each assessment, stating its specific purpose for the school within their assessment strategy.

Generating an Implementation Plan

Following the battery selection, the team endeavored to specify the timeline for administration. Table 8.1 shows a document that was used at Rosa Parks Elementary to create a master assessment plan, including purpose and timeline. If you do not have a similar document for your school or district, now is a good time to create one. We often find that a discussion around an assessment's purpose is very telling for how well it fits with the stated goals, as well

TABLE 8.1. Rosa Parks Elementary: Master Assessment Plan

Test	What it measures	Administrator	Grade levels	Administration schedule
PALS PreK	Early code-based skills	Teacher	Preschool	Fall, Spring
Expressive One-Word Picture Vocabulary Test	Expressive vocabulary	Teacher	Preschool–fifth grade	Fall, Spring
DIBELS	Decoding skills (phonemic awareness, phonics, and/or oral reading fluency, dependent on grade level)	Teacher	Kindergarten–fifth grade	Fall, Winter, Spring
Test of Word Reading Efficiency	Fluency in reading sight words and decoding non-words	Teacher	Second–fifth grade	Fall, Winter, Spring
Gates–MacGinitie Reading Test	Text comprehension skills (oral or reading)	Teacher (whole class)	Kindergarten–fifth grade	Fall, Spring
State Test	Text comprehension skills	TBD	Third–fifth grade	Spring

as the overall plan for instruction. At its core, data-driven instruction focuses on a clear and direct link between what is being measured and the overall purpose for instruction.

Next, the team generated a plan to bring the whole staff on board—one to genuinely make this a schoolwide, focused effort. In order to do so, it was clear that this would have to come into the spotlight, at the expense of other initiatives. This would require a doggedness on their part, but especially on the part of Principal Lansdowne to keep pushing the agenda forward and thus ensure that a cohesive approach is carried out. For example, at Rosa Parks Elementary, professional development (PD) had traditionally followed a path of serendipity. If funds came through, programs would be invited to the school to provide PD, often on short notice because the funds had to be spent within the academic year. At other times, PD followed district-level directives. However, PD was not driven by the instructional needs surfaced in the school's data. Principal Lansdowne wanted to make sure that grade-level team meetings naturally followed some of the schoolwide sessions that were scheduled into the year. Even more importantly, she wanted to make sure her own team met to understand key issues in order to best provide instructional support to teachers. Together, they crafted a three-pronged plan: leadership team meetings, school-level PD sessions, and grade-level team meeting topics for the fall, winter, and spring assessment periods. Their plan is in the box below.

With the plan outlined, the assessment team set dates and topics for both schoolwide PD sessions and grade-level team meetings in a calendar that was put into the written assessment plan. When they returned from summer break in July, Principal Lansdowne would ask the secretary to make a large version of the calendar for the teacher's lounge. From the very first day of school, there would be a clear infrastructure in place to support the work.

In almost every school there are mechanisms in place to ensure that teams of teachers meet regularly. Sometimes these meetings are highly effective, particularly when a teacher leader is guiding the session. However, it seems more common for such meetings to lack a clear goal or outcome. Generally the agenda is free-form, or perhaps develops in response to the latest issue that has popped up. When student concerns are raised, it is all too common for teachers to walk away from a team meeting without clear direction for next steps.

In our work, we have found that data meetings work best when planned a year or semester in advance. While this can seem impossible, there are common issues that arise every year. For example, it is fairly safe to schedule a meeting to discuss the results of an assessment a few weeks after the testing window. Indeed, as shown in Table 8.2, we encourage these meetings to be recorded on a master calendar along with the testing windows.

CRAFTING AN ASSESSMENT STRATEGY

1. Strike a team of key players.
2. Collectively generate a purpose statement for assessment.
3. Analyze the statement's goals in relation to current assessment practices.
4. Identify necessary assessment changes to realize goals.
5. Generate an implementation plan.

TABLE 8.2. Master Calendar for Data Meetings

Leadership team meetings	School-level professional development sessions	Grade-level team meetings
	Fall	

Fall data debrief meeting
• Patterns across the school
• Area of emphasis for each grade level
• Priorities for PD
• Identifying and allocating resources and materials
 	
Output: Action plan
	Understanding literacy data
	
	Topics
	• Types of assessments
	• What assessments tell us (what skills are measured—how this matches instruction)
	  ○ Using data to predict success
	  ○ Effective instructional strategies
	Activity
	• Looking at sample data (in grade-level groups)
	  ○ To determine priorities for the instructional core
	  ○ To form instructional groups
		Using spring data for instructional grouping that is focused on specific skills
		
		Output: Instructional groups
		
		Using fall data to shape the literacy block
		
		Output: Daily schedule for the literacy block with time for specific skills instruction based on needs identified in fall data
		
		Fall data for instructional grouping
		
		Output: New instructional groups based on fall scores
		
		Establishing procedures for the reading block
		
		Output: Several concrete procedures for having students move into groups and centers
		
		K0–K2: Focusing in on vocabulary instruction
		First–third grade: Focusing in on comprehension instruction
		
		Output: Identify one strategy that the grade level will decide to implement/refine

	Winter	
Winter data debrief meetings • Patterns within classrooms • Needs for literacy strands in specific classrooms *Output:* Action plan for supporting classroom teachers. May include walk-throughs, resources (push-in, staff assistant), materials, training	Using literacy data to target intervention Topics • Identifying specific student needs • Intervening within a curriculum • Progress monitoring	Winter data for instructional grouping *Output:* New instructional groups based on winter results Examining current centers to see if they are intentional and print based

(cont.)

TABLE 8.2. *(cont.)*

Leadership team meetings	School-level professional development sessions	Grade-level team meetings
	Winter *(cont.)*	
	Activity • Grade-level case discussions and whole-group share back	Using winter data to differentiate instructional centers *Output:* One differentiated center that is tied to print Reaching out to parents: Identifying children with low scores and low reading log participation to encourage home reading *Output:* Plan for reaching out to two specific families Using winter data to target a "double dose" *Output:* Plan for extra group to target students with decoding difficulties
	Spring	
Spring data debrief Reflection and planning for the upcoming year. • Progress made over the year • Growth areas • PD for following year • Scheduling for following year • Allocating resources for following year *Output:* Action plan for following year	Differentiating instruction Topics • Understanding the academic growth of ELLs • Adapting the assessment system to identify instructional needs of struggling students • Engaging and pushing high-performing students	Using spring data to monitor progress: What is working, who isn't responding to intervention *Output:* Small instructional groups with specific ideas for approaching content through different learning style/modality Sharing data with families *Output:* Ideas for sharing results at parent–teacher conferences Using spring data to identify students who are not responding to intervention *Output:* Timeline and plan for follow-up

Your school or district should consider how instruction is discussed among school leaders and within PD sessions and smaller team meetings. How will key players stay abreast of issues that arise from the data? How can PD coordinate with smaller, more targeted discussions? If your plan does not coordinate across levels, now is the time to align efforts.

Figure 8.1 shows a list of sample topics for instructional team meetings that map onto common instructional challenges throughout the year that can be used as a starting point for advance planning. A clear take-away or action step should be part of the agenda for any team meeting. Many of the activities in this book would serve such a purpose. For example, in Chapter 6, there is a form for teachers to record their instructional approach (Form 6.2), including allocating time for specific instructional components. The challenge is for teachers to identify an instructional priority and then revisit their plan for allocating time. This activity could easily become the basis for a team meeting.

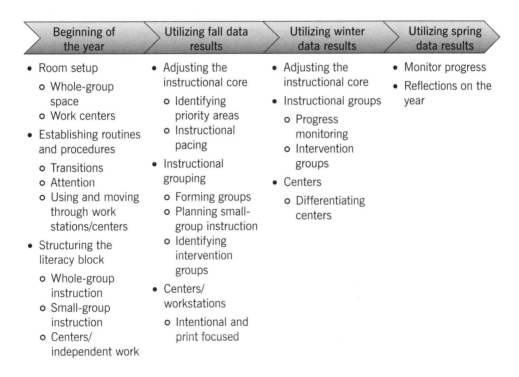

Beginning of the year	Utilizing fall data results	Utilizing winter data results	Utilizing spring data results

• Room setup
  o Whole-group space
  o Work centers
• Establishing routines and procedures
  o Transitions
  o Attention
  o Using and moving through work stations/centers
• Structuring the literacy block
  o Whole-group instruction
  o Small-group instruction
  o Centers/ independent work
	• Adjusting the instructional core
	  o Identifying priority areas
	  o Instructional pacing
	• Instructional grouping
	  o Forming groups
	  o Planning small-group instruction
	  o Identifying intervention groups
	• Centers/ workstations
	  o Intentional and print focused
		• Adjusting the instructional core
		• Instructional groups
		  o Progress monitoring
		  o Intervention groups
		• Centers
		  o Differentiating centers
			• Monitor progress
			• Reflections on the year

FIGURE 8.1. Sample topics and timelines for grade-level team meetings.

Step 2: Leading the Implementation
of a New Assessment Strategy

For the educator leading this process of strengthening literacy instruction, in some ways forming a team and crafting a plan is the easy part. The next step toward lasting instructional improvement involves moving to implementation at the whole-school level. For the school leader, it is crucial to recognize that implementing a new plan for assessment must include significant attention to when and (especially) how information will be disseminated to teachers and staff, and the important topics for discussion and presentation.

Initial Introduction/Training: Who and When?

Two practical decisions central to leading the implementation process in a deliberate, focused manner include who will provide the initial training on the new assessments (the why and how) and when this will take place. For example, in previous years, teachers at Rosa Parks Elementary learned about changes when they were scheduled to attend training seminars, such as those on how to administer new assessments. These seminars were often presented by representatives of the testing company, and therefore did not include discussion of how the assessment fit into the school's strategy or curriculum. All too often, the staff walked away unclear as to why the new assessments had been adopted and how it might help their practice and their students' performance. For this reason, based on our work at Rosa Parks Elementary and in other buildings, we have at least two strong recommendations as you set out:

1. The assessment team is well positioned to lead meetings that focus on explaining the type of assessments to be used and their intended purpose within the school's mission and instructional strategy.
2. These informational meetings should take place in the spring, *before* any training in administering new measures, which should take place the next fall.

The emphasis on the purpose of assessment is central to the fidelity of the implementation of the new battery, as many problems, including misuse and mistrust of scores, arise when tests are not sufficiently understood conceptually. For example, in the initial meeting at Rosa Parks Elementary, Franny, Carter's teacher, took issue with his low vocabulary score, in part because it felt like a negative, potentially inaccurate, evaluation of Carter's abilities.

In subsequent discussion among those at the meeting and drawing on many examples provided by colleagues, the purpose of the assessment—strictly to identify students who might be at risk for future reading difficulties in order to provide them increased instructional supports—was delineated. Following this, the test seemed more worthwhile to her.

Data as a Stepping Stone to Instruction

If you are leading this process, once the data has been gathered, the danger is that it feels like the job is done and the process was a success. All too often, as we heard about at Rosa Parks Elementary, score reports are generated, the information is available and circulated to all parties, and the buck stops there. In these settings, the data does not become central to discussions about instruction and is not embedded in PD activities. Very often, teachers focus only on individual students, rather than taking a step back and identifying overarching patterns in their aggregate data to inform their overall instructional approach. And, understandably, teachers typically look at the scores of their own students; very rarely are they engaged in discussion of schoolwide trends beyond those that focus on the results on outcome assessments, such as statewide accountability measures (see Chapter 3). As a departure from standard practices, we encourage schoolwide data sharing as a *first* step of score analysis at the completion of an assessment cycle. We have found discussing the data generated from screening assessments often reduces the tendency to shift blame downward for low scores (e.g., "if the first-grade teachers had done their job . . . "), as staff gains awareness of challenges faced at every step of a child's journey as a reader. We also encourage schools to put together a table that summarizes the percentage of students at risk in a particular skill area across grade levels. Right away, this starts a collective discussion of the needs and priorities of the school population. Table 8.3 shows rates of risk for the readers at Rosa Parks Elementary by grade level. What do you notice about patterns in their scores?

Identifying Instructional Priorities

In looking at the data, conversations should center on two comprehensive, guiding questions: What do these results tell us about our instruction? In what ways do we need to adjust our strategy and approach? An important goal of this process should be to identify a common priority area that can be a focus across the school and involving all stakeholders—from the bus drivers and cafeteria workers, to the reading specialist. For this focus, scores are just a starting

TABLE 8.3. Percentage of Students Identified At Risk by Literacy Skill: Rosa Parks Elementary

Grade level	Phonemic awareness	Phonics	Fluency	Vocabulary	Comprehension
		Literacy component			
K2	63%	17%		83%	40%
First	19%	73%	N/A	70%	50%
Second		40%	71%	79%	65%
Third		41%	68%	86%	78%

point: the goal is to provide the best possible instructional environment for children, from their very first interaction with school in the morning to their last words as they hop off the bus at the end of the day. For example, when Principal Lansdowne led a discussion around the results presented above, teachers noticed right away that many children struggle in code-based skills, although the proportion of students decreases with every grade level. However, a high number of students struggled persistently, through the grades, with vocabulary, and actually it appeared that this became an increasing problem with time. The staff then came to agreement to focus on vocabulary schoolwide.

Setting a Goal and Designing a Strategy

Of course, having identified a priority area for instruction, a key step in the process of leading data-driven instruction is to then create a clear and compelling tangible goal toward improving student outcomes, and a strategy to meet that goal. For Principal Lansdowne and her team at Rosa Parks Elementary, this means setting a measureable target in vocabulary for each grade level and talking about how they were going to meet that goal. The actual steps a school (or district) takes in reaching a goal will vary. However, when a school unites around a common instructional goal—especially one that is pulled from data—a strong foundation is set for improving student achievement. Research shows, for example, that specific goals lead to higher performance than just encouraging someone to do a better job (Locke & Latham, 1990). Goals direct actions toward relevant tasks, motivate people to work harder and persist longer in their contribution, and lead to greater personal learning and development (Latham & Locke, 2002). Entire books are devoted to goal-setting processes for schools and districts toward school achievement. Two good resources for thinking more deeply about setting goals are the PELP

Problem-Solving Framework (Childress & Marietta, 2008) and the 2009 book *Leading for Equity*, by Stacey Childress, Denis Doyle, and David Thomas.

So what happened, exactly, at Rosa Parks Elementary? Once vocabulary building was identified as an instructional priority, the staff brainstormed how the whole school could be involved in promoting it; this took place at an open meeting with all staff, including janitors and secretaries. The ideas generated to improve vocabulary schoolwide were fun and challenging, ranging from changing the wording of morning announcements (e.g., *"Salutations, scholars! The proclamation of the day is . . . "*), to holding a vocabulary bee. The best ideas, as determined through vigorous debate and voting process, were then chosen for implementation. One of the strategies selected was a schoolwide, common thematic science unit on weather that could be taught at all grade levels in November. Another was that the displays outside in the school's halls could become a source of discussion for anybody who walked by, and, finally, older students would have an opportunity to work with some of the younger students at the school. The librarian could focus on weather-related books as well as fiction stories with weather themes to show students and for read-aloud during library time. Parents could also be involved in the unit through newsletters, invitations to student presentations, and events at the school.

In turn, the leadership team held its own meetings around this newly identified priority, setting goals for their own work. If school staff were going to focus on vocabulary, then support was needed. Any change in focus requires coordinated changes in a number of areas, including PD and how teachers and the principal use their time. The leadership team would be in charge of managing these changes.

As we enact instructional change, it is important to bear in mind that the skills that are most difficult for our students—and therefore very likely to surface as a schoolwide priority—are often the hard to measure and hard to move meaning-based skills, such as vocabulary, background knowledge, and comprehension (see Chapter 2). In turn, it is important to keep in mind that we may not see immediate results in screening scores, as we might when focusing on discrete skills. Discussion is needed to find a clear and compelling goal. Maybe a school decides students in every grade level will learn a certain number of words from the Academic Word List (Coxhead, 2000), or read a certain number of books. Perhaps the goal will be to see a 10% increase in the overall school's score on a vocabulary assessment. Even when results are modest, we should not give up, but understand that the data tells us our jobs are far from over. Instead, we need to keep working, guided in our efforts by progress monitoring assessments, which are far better suited to showing incremental progress.

At this point in the process, leading change becomes about cycles of analysis to promote continuous improvement. We will always need to monitor and revise our strategy, and can always create more challenging goals.

The Data-Driven Journey: A Self-Evaluation

At the beginning of this book, we set out on a journey to create a new relationship with data. Rather than focusing on specific tests and trying to move single scores, we argue that educators need to keep sight of the genuine goal of literacy instruction—to promote students' knowledge base, independent and collaborative inquiry about the world, and their communication skills. In this vein, the very best instruction is robust and balanced, but is also targeted to the group of learners in the building or the classroom. The overarching goal, then, is to use assessments as a tool or platform for instructional improvement. In so doing, we remind ourselves that assessments are only as good as the way they are implemented and their scores interpreted. And while test scores direct our attention, they do not provide all the answers for instruction. And we note that good assessment batteries measure all the important components of literacy and create a springboard for instructional change inspired by best practices—it is not the assessment itself that does this.

We hope that by the time you put this book down you will have some questions about your own approach and perhaps even have identified some shortcomings of the current strategy in place—asking yourself how your data fits your students and your pressing issues and how well it is used to inform instruction—but definitely some potential solutions as well. You will recognize the different types of assessment tools, as well as seeing the importance of measuring various skills. You will use data to differentiate for your schools, your classrooms, and your individual students, targeting instruction to the specific identified needs.

Therefore, as a final piece, we leave you with a self-evaluation tool (Form 8.1, at the end of the chapter) to guide you in understanding how well data-driven instruction is implemented in your particular context. This tool should help you gauge your progress and focus your attention on key areas of need within your system. After all, the more we learn about ourselves, the more we can strive for continuous improvement. Data helps us set our "north star," the ultimate dreams and goals we have for our children. We may never reach the star, but we can feel confident that we are moving in the right direction.

Data-Driven Instruction: Self-Evaluation Tool

Use the following rubric to evaluate your school on how well you are implementing data-driven instruction.

	1	2	3	4	5
Scheduling	Few teachers provide assessment results to school or district leaders	Many teachers do not complete the assessment battery in a timely fashion; scores are missing for several students, and/or subtests	Most teachers complete testing in a timely fashion, although some are predictably late; or, data are missing on several students, particularly high-risk students (e.g., ELLs, special education, students with many absences)	All teachers complete testing in a timely fashion, although there is no system in place to catch absent students, resulting in missing information on some high-risk students (e.g., ELLs, special education, students with many absences)	All teachers complete testing in a timely fashion; every effort is made to ensure that all students are tested through a clear make-up system
Administration	Scores difficult to interpret due to inconsistencies in administration; may be administered by volunteer tutors, paraprofessionals, or others who have limited or no training in the measure, or teacher-led administration may reveal fears and mistrust	There is lingering confusion around testing procedures and/or scoring, resulting in nonstandard practice and some questionable scores	Some teachers do not administer assessments to their own students and may be completely unfamiliar with the measure; not all key staff have been trained in administration	Test administrators received training on testing procedures, but are not yet fully familiar and comfortable with measures	Test administrators clearly understand rules and follow standardized testing procedures; teachers administer formative assessments to their own students

(cont.)

FORM 8.1 *(page 2 of 2)*

	1	2	3	4	5
Reporting	Each teacher has his or her own way to report data; not all classrooms report the same scores; data not easily accessed by instructional leaders	Reporting systems vary by grade level and/or classroom and are not consistent throughout the school	There is a common system of reporting scores, although it is not consistently used by all teachers	Teachers use a common system of reporting scores, although it is not centrally organized and may be difficult to access	Teachers use a common system of reporting scores that are collected and organized in a central system
Assessment literacy	Teachers focus on literacy assessments as an evaluation tool resulting in fear and mistrust; some teachers may inflate scores to protect their professional image	Assessments seen solely as a vehicle for placing children in groups or identifying them as "above" or "below" grade level	Understanding of assessments varies by measure and by teacher, although there is limited discussion of the specific skills being measured	Most teachers have a general understanding of the assessments, although they may not be clear on how the specific skills being assessed fit into a comprehensive and balanced literacy block	Teachers understand what literacy components are measured and what results tell about students; they can translate results into teaching strategies that are evidence based
Data meetings	Data are not discussed	There is no system or schedule in place to discuss data, although there are pockets of professionals who discuss results	Some teachers meet regularly to discuss data, but data meetings are not consistent across the school; data meetings may be frequently canceled or dominated by more immediate issues	Regular meetings are scheduled to discuss student results, although the focus of the meetings are not systematic; meetings sometimes canceled or interrupted	Regular and systematic meetings are scheduled to discuss student results; meetings are considered "sacred"; meetings focus on instructional practice and intervention
Application	Assessment results are reported for compliance reasons only; no consideration of results is used in planning instruction	Teachers re-create assessment procedures as their main strategy of addressing results	Teachers use experience and intuition to modify instruction based on assessment results, with limited application to the literacy block or targeted interventions	Assessment results consistently used to form instructional groups, but results are not connected to evidence-based practices	Assessment results are used to strategically inform core instruction and intervention using evidence-based practices

References

Alexander, P. A., & Jetton, T. L. (2000). Learning from text: A multidimensional and developmental perspective. In R. Barr, M. Kamil, P. Mosenthal, & P. D. Pearson (Eds.), *Handbook of reading research* (Vol. 3, pp. 285–310). New York: Longman.

Anderson, R. C. (2004). Role of the reader's schema in comprehension, learning, and memory. In R. B. Ruddell & N. J. Unrau (Eds.), *Theoretical models and processes of reading* (5th ed., pp. 594–606). Newark, DE: International Reading Association.

August, D., & Shanahan, T. (2006). *Developing literacy in second-language learners: Report of the National Literacy Panel on Language-Minority Children and Youth.* Mahwah, NJ: Erlbaum.

Baumann, J. F., Kame'enui, E. J., & Ash, G. (2003). Research on vocabulary instruction: Voltaire redux. In J. Flood, D. Lapp, J. R. Squire, & J. Jensen (Eds.), *Handbook of research on teaching the English language arts* (pp. 752–785). Mahwah, NJ: Erlbaum.

Bear, D., Invernizzi, M., Templeton, S., & Johnston, F. (2011). *Words their way: Word study for phonics, vocabulary and spelling instruction* (5th ed.). Boston: Allyn & Bacon.

Beaver, J. M. (2006). *Teacher guide: Developmental Reading Assessment, Grades K–3* (2nd ed.). Parsippany, NJ: Pearson Education.

Beck, I. L., McKeown, M. G., & Kucan, L. (2002). *Bringing words to life: Robust vocabulary instruction.* New York: Guilford Press.

Biancarosa, G., & Snow, C. E. (2006). *Reading Next:A vision for action and research in middle and high school literacy* (2nd ed.). Washington, DC: Alliance for Excellent Education. Retrieved from *www.all4ed.org/publications/ReadingNext/ReadingNext.pdf.*

Biemiller, A., & Slonim, N. (2001). Estimating root word vocabulary growth in normative and advantaged populations: Evidence for a common sequence of vocabulary acquisition. *Journal of Educational Psychology, 93*(3), 498–520.

Boudett, K. P., City, E. A., & Murnane, R. J. (2005). *Data wise: A step-by-step guide to using assessment results to improve teaching and learning.* Cambridge, MA: Harvard Education Press.

Bransford, J. D. (2004). Schema activation and schema acquisition: Comments on Richard C. Anderson's remarks. In R. B. Ruddell & N. J. Unrau (Eds.), *Theoretical models and processes of reading* (5th ed., pp. 607–619). Newark, DE: International Reading Association.

Cartwright, K. B. (Ed.). (2008). *Literacy processes: Cognitive flexibility in learning and teaching.* New York: Guilford Press.

Chall, J. S. (1996). *Stages of reading development.* Orlando, FL: Harcourt Brace.

Chall, J. S., & Jacobs, V. A. (2003). The classic study on poor children's fourth-grade slump. *American Educator, 27*(1), 14–15.

Childress, S., Doyle, D. P., & Thomas, D. A. (2009). *Leading for equity: The pursuit of excellence in Montgomery County Public Schools.* Cambridge, MA: Harvard Education Press.

Childress, S., & Marietta, G. (2008). *A problem-solving approach to designing and implementing a strategy to improve performance.* Boston: Harvard Business School.

Clay, M. (1993). *An observation survey: Of early literacy achievement.* Portsmouth, NH: Heinemann.

Connor, C. M. (2011). Child characteristics-instruction interactions: Implications for students' literacy skills development in the early grades. In S. B. Neuman & D. K. Dickinson (Eds.), *Handbook of early literacy research* (Vol. 3, pp. 256–279). New York: Guilford Press.

Coxhead, A. (2000). A new academic word list. *TESOL Quarterly, 34*(2), 213–238.

Crosson, A. C., & Lesaux, N. K. (2010). Revisiting assumptions about the relationship of fluent reading to comprehension: Spanish-speakers' text-reading fluency in English. *Reading and Writing: An Interdisciplinary Journal, 23,* 475–494.

Crosson, A. C., Lesaux, N. K., & Martiniello, M. (2008). Factors that influence comprehension of connectives among language minority children from Spanish-speaking backgrounds. *Applied Psycholinguistics, 29,* 603–624.

Dickinson, D. K., & Tabors, P. O. (2001). *Beginning literacy with Language: Young children learning at home and school.* Baltimore, MD: Brookes.

Duke, N. K., Pressley, M., & Hilden, K. (2004). Difficulties with reading comprehension. In C. A. Stone, E. R. Silliman, B. J. Ehren, & K. Apel (Eds.), *Handbook of language and literacy* (pp. 501–520). New York: Guilford Press.

Dunn, L. M., & Dunn, L. M. (1997). *Peabody Picture Vocabulary Test* (3rd ed.). Circle Pines, MN: American Guidance Service.

Education Quality and Accountability Office. (2010). *Ontario student achievement: EQAO's Provincial Elementary School Report on the Results of the 2009–2010 Assessments of Reading, Writing and Mathematics, Primary Division (Grades 1–3) and Junior Division (Grades 4–6).* Retrieved from: *www.eqao.com/pdf_e/10/EQAO_ProvincialReport_Elementary2010.pdf.*

Fountas, I. C., & Pinnell, G. S. (2007a). *Fountas and Pinnell benchmark assessment system 1: Grades K–2, levels A–N.* Portsmouth, NH: Heinemann.

Fountas, I. C., & Pinnell, G. S. (2007b). *Fountas and Pinnell benchmark assessment system 2: Grades 3–8, levels L–Z.* Portsmouth, NH: Heinemann.

Fuchs, D., & Fuchs, L. (2005, September/October). Responsiveness-to-intervention: A blueprint for practitioners, policymakers, and parents. *Teaching Exceptional Children,* 57–61.

Fuchs, L. S. & Fuchs, D. (2006). Implementing RTI to identify LD. *Perspectives on Dyslexia, 32*(1), 39–43.

Gándara, P., & Rumberger, R. W. (2003). Seeking equity in the education of California's English learners. *Teachers College Record, 106*(10), 2032–2056.

Gaskins, I. W., Satlow, E., & Pressley, M. (2007). Executive control of reading comprehension in the elementary school. In L. Meltzer (Ed.), *Executive function in education: From theory to practice* (pp. 194–215). New York: Guilford Press.

George, J. C. (1959). *My side of the mountain.* London, UK: Puffin Books.

Good, R. H., & Kaminski, R. A. (Eds.). (2002). *Dynamic indicators of basic early literacy skills* (6th ed.). Eugene, OR: Institute for the Development of Educational Achievement.

Good, R. H., Simmons, D. S., Kame'enui, E. J., Kaminski, R. A., & Wallin, J. (2002). *Summary of decision rules for intensive, strategic, and benchmark instructional recommendations in kindergarten through third grade* (Tech. Rep. No. 11). Eugene: University of Oregon.

Goodman, K. (2006). *The truth about DIBELS: What it is, what it does.* Portsmouth, NH: Heinemann.

Fisher, D., Frey, N., & Rothenberg, C. (2008). *Content area conversations: How to plan lesson-based discussions for diverse language learners.* Alexandria, VA: Association for Supervision and Curriculum Development.

Fuchs, D., Mock, D., Morgan, P. L., & Young, C. L. (2003). Responsiveness-to-intervention: Definitions, evidence, and implications for the learning disabilities construct. *Learning Disabilities Research and Practice, 18,* 157–171.

Hall, S. (2006). *I've Dibel'd, now what? Designing interventions with DIBELS Data.* Frederik, CO: Sopris West.

Hart, B., & Risley, T. R. (1995). *Meaningful differences in the everyday experience of young American children.* Baltimore: Brookes.

Hasbrouck, J., & Tindal, G. A. (2006). Oral reading fluency norms: A valuable assessment tool for reading teachers. *Reading Teacher, 59*(7), 636–644.

Hosp, M. K., Hosp, J. L., & Howell, K. W. (2007). *The ABCs of CBM: A practical guide to curriculum-based measurement.* New York: Guilford Press.

Jean, M., & Geva, E. (2009). The development of vocabulary in English as a second language children and its role in predicting word recognition ability. *Applied Psycholinguistics, 30,* 153–185.

Kintsch, W., & Kintsch, E. (2005). Comprehension. In S. G. Paris & S. A. Stahl (Eds.), *Children's reading comprehension and assessment* (pp. 71–92). Mahwah, NJ: Erlbaum.

Klingner, J., Soltero-Gonzalez, L., & Lesaux, N. K. (2010). RTI for English-language learners. In M. Y. Lipson & K. K. Wixson (Eds.), *Successful approaches to RTI: Collaborative practices for improving K–12 literacy* (pp. 134–162). Newark, DE: International Reading Association.

Koretz, D. (2008). *Measuring up: What educational testing really tells us.* Cambridge, MA: Harvard University Press.

Latham, G., & Locke, E. (2002). Building a practically useful theory of goal setting and task motivation. *American Psychologist, 57,* 705–717.

Lesaux, N. K., Crosson, A. C., Kieffer, M. J., & Pierce, M. (2010). Uneven profiles: Language minority learners' word reading, vocabulary, and reading comprehension skills. *Journal of Applied Developmental Psychology, 31,* 475–483.

Lesaux, N. K. & Kieffer, M. J. (2010). Exploring sources of reading comprehension difficulties among language minority learners and their classmates in early adolescence. *American Educational Research Journal, 47*, 596–632.

Lesaux, N. K., Kieffer, M. J., Faller, S. E., & Kelley, J. G. (2010). The effectiveness and ease of implementation of an academic vocabulary intervention for linguistically diverse students in urban middle schools. *Reading Research Quarterly, 45*(2), 196–228.

Lipson, M. Y., & Wixson, K. K. (2003). *Assessment and instruction of reading and writing difficulty.* Boston: Allyn & Bacon.

Lipson, M. Y., & Wixson, K. K. (Eds.). (2010). *Successful approaches to RTI: Collaborative practices for improving K–12 literacy.* Newark, DE: International Reading Association.

Locke, E. A., & Latham, G. P. (1990). *A theory of goal setting and task performance.* Englewood Cliffs, NJ: Prentice-Hall.

MacGinitie, W., MacGinitie, R., Maria, K., & Dreyer, L.G. (2000). *Gates–MacGinitie Reading Test. (4th ed.).* Itasca, IL: Riverside Publishing Company.

Mancilla-Martinez, J., & Lesaux, N. K. (2011). The gap between Spanish-speakers' word reading and word knowledge: A longitudinal study. *Child Development, 82*, 1544–1560.

McKenna, M. C., & Stahl, K. A. D. (2009). *Assessment for reading instruction* (2nd ed.). New York: Guilford Press.

Murphy, P., Wilkinson, I. G., Soter, A. O., Hennessey, M. N., & Alexander, J. F. (2009). Examining the effects of classroom discussion on students' comprehension of text: A meta-analysis. *Journal of Educational Psychology, 101*, 740–764.

National Center for Education Statistics. (2010). *The nation's report card.* Retrieved from *nces. ed.gov/nationsreportcard.*

National Center on Response to Intervention. (n.d.). What is RTI? Retrieved September 21, 2011, from *rti4success.org.*

National Institute of Child Health and Human Development. (2000). *Teaching children to read: An evidence-based assessment of the scientific research literature on reading and its implications for reading instruction: Report of the National Reading Panel* (NIH Publication No. 00-4769). Washington, DC: U.S. Government Printing Office.

Orfield, G., & Lee, C. (2005). *Why segregation matters: Poverty and educational inequality.* Cambridge, MA: Civil Rights Project at Harvard University. Retrieved from *civilrightsproject.ucla.edu.*

Paris, S. G. (2005). Reinterpreting the development of reading skills. *Reading Research Quarterly, 40*(2), 184–202.

Passel, J. S. & Cohn, V. (2008). *U.S. Population Projections: 2005–2050.* Washington, DC: Pew Hispanic Center.

Pilkey, D. (1997). *The adventures of captain underpants.* New York: Scholastic.

Pressley, M. (2006). *Reading instruction that works: The case for balanced teaching* (3rd ed.). New York: Guilford Press.

Raikes, H., Pan, B. A., Luze, G., Tamis-LeMonda, C. S., Brooks-Gunn, J., Constantine, J., et al. (2006). Mother–child bookreading in low-income families: Correlates and outcomes during the first three years of life. *Child Development, 77*(4), 924–953.

RAND Reading Study Group. (2002). *Reading for understanding: Toward a R&D program in reading*. Arlington, VA: Author.

Sáenz, L. (2008). *Using CBM to progress monitor English language learners*. Webinar delivered March 11, 2008. Washington, DC: National Center on Student Progress Monitoring. Retrieved from *www.studentprogress.org/weblibrary.asp*.

Sattler, J. M. (2008). *Assessment of children: Cognitive foundations* (5th ed.). San Diego, CA: Sattler.

Scarborough, H. S. (2002). Connecting early language and literacy to later reading (dis)abilities: Evidence, theory, and practice. In S. Neuman & D. Dickinson (Eds.), *Handbook of early literacy research* (Vol. 1, pp. 97–110). New York: Guilford Press.

Schmidley, D. (2001). *The Foreign-Born Population in the United States: March 2002. Population characteristics. Current population reports*. Washington, DC: U.S. Department of Commerce, Economics and Statistics Administration, U.S. Census Bureau.

Shapiro, E. S., Zigmond, N., Wallace, T., & Marston, D. (2011). *Models for implementing response to intervention: Tools, outcomes, and implications*. New York: Guilford Press.

Shields, M. K., & Behrman, R. E. (2004). Children of immigrant families: Analysis and recommendations. *Future of Children, 14*(2), 4–17.

Snow, C. E., Burns, M. S., & Griffin, P. (Eds.). (1998). *Preventing reading difficulties in young children*. Washington, DC: National Academy Press.

Snow, C. E., & Juel, C. (2005). Teaching children to read: What do we know about how to do it? In M. J. Snowling & C. Hulme (Eds.), *The Science of Reading: A Handbook* (pp. 501–520). Oxford, UK: Blackwell.

Stahl, S. A., & Nagy, W. E. (2006). *Teaching word meanings*. Mahwah, NJ: Erlbaum.

Thorndike, R. M., & Thorndike-Christ, T. M. (2009). *Measurement and evaluation in psychology and education* (8th ed.). Englewood Cliffs, NJ: Prentice-Hall.

Torgesen, J. K., Wagner, R. K., & Rashotte, C. A. (1999). *Test of Word Reading Efficiency (TOWRE)*. Austin, TX: Pro-Ed.

UK Department of Education. (2010). *First Release: Key State 2 Attainment by Pupil Characteristics in England 2009/2010*. Retrieved from *www.education.gov.uk/rsgateway/DB/SFR/s000972/sfr35-2010.pdf*.

Zehler, A., Fleischman, H., Hopstock, P., Stephenson, T., Pendzick, M., & Sapru, S. (2003). *Policy report: Summary of findings related to LEP and SPED-LEP students* (Report submitted to U.S. Department of Education, Office of English Language Acquisition, Language Enhancement, and Academic Achievement of Limited English Proficient Students). Arlington, VA: Development Associates.

Index

An *f* following a page number indicates a figure;
a *t* following a page number indicates a table.